Geo-Political Road Kill
Book #8

OTHER PUBLISHED BOOKS

BY

AKIN O. AKINDELE

1. THE MILITARY FRANCHISE
2. THE GENIUS OF SOCCER
3. UTOPIA, EUPHORIA, MYOPIA
4. INSPIRATION
5. WINNING FORMULA
6. GREED INCORPORATED
7. PEOPLE, PASSION, PURPOSE (AMAZING GRACE)
8. GEO-POLITICAL ROAD KILL

* copies of these books may be purchased through all major on-line bookstores (Xlibris.com; Amazon.com; Borders.com; Barnesandnoble.com; or by calling 1-888-795-4274 ext. 876) or through The Akindele Foundation at The Akindele Foundation Building 18833-45 Detroit, MI 48213 (email—*taf@yahoo.com*) or c/o P.O.BOX 6285 Vallejo, CA 94591.

* PROCEEDS FROM ALL OF THESE BOOKS HAVE AND CONTINUE TO BE DEDICATED TO THE ACTIVITIES OF THE AKINDELE FOUNDATION BOTH IN THE USA AND AFRICA

Geo-Political Road Kill Book #8

Revisiting Africa's Failing Quest For Liberty, Justice & Progress

Dr. Akin O. Akindele

To order additional copies of this book, contact:
Xlibris Corporation
1-888-795-4274
www.Xlibris.com
Orders@Xlibris.com
57444

CONTENTS

"When you change the way you look at things, the things you look at markedly change"—Wisdom of the TAO

AKIN O. AKINDELE'S Book #8 **(GEO-POLITICAL ROAD KILL)** is the third volume in a thematic trilogy about Africa's (and more specifically Nigeria's) socio-political evolution, challenges and missed opportunities post colonial rule (which ended for most of the countries in Africa in the early 1960s).

As a follow up edition to **THE MILITARY FRANCHISE (1993) and PEOPLE, PASSION, PURPOSE—Book #7 (2008),** this Book attempts to build on these two other Books and my other related initiatives on this subject.

Combined, these three Books arguably constitute (some of the early drafts of Africa's recent history and) A COMPREHENSIVE PROPHYLACTIC (if you will) offered with love TO HOPEFULLY INSPIRE THE NEXT GENERATION OF LEADERS.

More importantly, these Books help to refocus attention on our collective quest of finally overcoming the insidious Cancer known as **'AFRICAN DEMO-KRAZY' (or post-colonial hangover).**

A SAMPLING OF WHAT PEOPLE ARE SAYING ABOUT THE AUTHOR

(1) **On Akindele's philanthropic efforts**:-

"Lawyer Akindele . . . we appreciate your large consignment of New . . . books . . . Such philanthropic gesture will definitely inspire the students . . . to emulate you . . ."
> —**Principal, Egirioke High School. NIGERIA (2004)**

"Thanks for the donated automobile . . ."
> —**Children's (Cancer) Hospital, USA (1996) (1999) & (2002)**

(2) **On his courageous Book, THE MILITARY FRANCHISE**:-

"The Military Franchise could not have come at a more auspicious Time . . . like a true nationalist the Author urges faith in place of Despair and believes there is a bright light at the end of the dark Political tunnel . . . the command of language and the compelling Logic of the author (makes) the book a compelling read . . ."
> —**TELL MAGAZINE, August 29, 1994**

". . . extolled Akindele's courage and described his effort as a Commitment to a noble cause which could bail Nigeria out of the scandalized and vandalized status . . . bestowed on her."
> —**SUNDAY GUARDIAN, January .15, 1994**

"The Military Franchise can best be described as an excursion into issues and ideas that are dominating contemporary Africa and Nigerian political discourse . . . (articulated by Akin O. Akindele) . . . with perhaps a rare language style of a combination of poetry and prose that is richly laced with humor . . ."
> —**THE NIGERIAN ECONOMIST, January 24, 1994**

(3) **On his continuing quest for international economic justice and fair play** which was brilliantly articulated in his sixth Book, **GREED INCORPORATED**:-

"Akindele employs his rich experience and in-depth knowledge in labor management, human relation, (and) economic analysis and as an Attorney . . . Philosopher and Poet. He theorizes on the modern Community . . . and the concept of . . . economic rights and social Justice . . ."

—**GUARDIAN May 2, 2005**

(4) On his inspirational Book, THE WINNING FORMULA:—

"The Author's language is down to earth, unpretentious and amazingly humble"

—**GUARDIAN April 25, 2005**

(5) On Akindele's general progressive posture and commitment to the cause of socio-political justice (everywhere)

"I on behalf of myself and our organization thank the Akindele Foundation immensely and commend your courage, energy and effort . . ."

—**Dr. Beko Ransome-Kuti, Chairman, Campaign for Democracy (CD) October 22, 1993**

". . . Thank you also for your continued support with the Wayne County Neighborhood Legal Services Children's Law Center, and for your faith in the city of Detroit."

—**Honorable Dennis W. Archer, Mayor, City of Detroit March12, 1997**

Lawyer Akin O. Akindele as a newly licensed legal practitioner in 1985—looking forward to his role as an advocate and an officer of the court in a just society governed by the rule of law. Well the quest for that JUST SOCIETY continues . . .

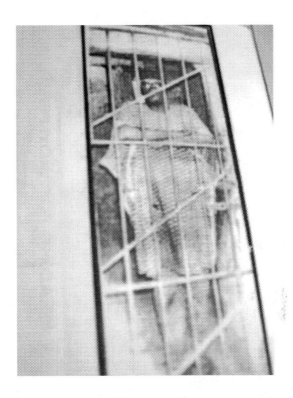

1996 PHOTO OF CHIEF GANI FAWEHINMI WHILE IN DETENTION IN BAUCHI PRISON FOR DARING TO SPEAK OUT FOR THE CAUSE OF JUSTICE.

The irrepressible Chief Gani Fawehinmi and other patriots blazed the trail in employing legal and other forms of social activism to steer the country and its often corrupt and indifferent leadership toward the path of righteousness and the RULE OF LAW.

For him and similar STATESMEN of his generation (like Professor Wole Soyinka, Alhaji Balarabe Musa, and others) it has been about forty (40) years of tireless activism, perseverance and SACRIFICE.

Apart from Falana, Keyamo and a few of my able contemporaries in the pro-democracy and justice movement who have apparently remained steadfast, focused and uncorrupted by the lure of temporal gains, not many in my (and the upcoming) generation have effectively distinguished themselves with the same level of commitment, creativity and personal sacrifice needed to move this process along more rapidly.

DEDICATION

The loneliest and most awe inspiring form of GREATNESS is SACRIFICE.

THIS BOOK WAS INSPIRED BY AND DEDICATED TO THE ENDURING LEGACIES OF THE FOLLOWING SOCIO-POLITICAL GIANTS (AND OTHERS OF THEIR IMMENSE CALIBER) WHO INDIVIDUALLY SACRIFICED SO MUCH SO THAT SO MANY OTHERS MAY BETTER ENJOY THE GIFT OF LIFE, LIBERTY AND THE PURSUIT OF HAPPYNESS;

CHIEF OBAFEMI AWOLOWO
ALHAJI AMINU KANO
MAJOR EMEKA NZEOGWU
PRESIDENT THOMAS SANKARA
MAHATMA GHANDI
HARRIET TAUBMAN
MINISTER MALCOLM X
REVEREND MARTIN LUTHER KING JR.
ABRAHAM LINCOLN
FELA & BEKO KUTI
TAI SOLARIN
PROFESSOR AYODELE AWOJOBI
MALAM BALARABE MUSA
PRESIDENT MANDELA
CHIEF ANTHONY ENAHORO
CHIEF GANI FAWEHINMI (SAN/SAM)
PROFESSOR WOLE SOYINKA

(& A NUMBER OF OTHERS EQUALLY WORTHY OF MENTION)

ACKNOWLEDGEMENTS

I acknowledge and again celebrate the profoundly inspired life lived by my late father, High Chief Funsho Akindele, the late Aro of Iyin Ekiti who positively impacted so many lives during his rather short journey.

The world was made that much poorer as a result of his passing. Thankfully, his examples endure. Those unmistakable giant markers continue to inspire and guide.

So to those who have lost loved ones whose exemplary lives they would have loved to share with the world, this one is for you.

AUTHOR'S BIOGRAPHICAL

Attended, Christ's School (Nigeria)
Attended Federal School of Arts & Science (Nigeria)
Attended Ibadan Polytechnic (Nigeria)
Graduate, Bachelor of Laws, (Nigeria)
Graduate, Barrister at Law, (Nigeria)
Graduate, Master of Laws (Canada)
Graduate, Special (Juris) Doctoral Program (USA)
Licensed Attorney (USA)
Barrister & Solicitor of the Federal Supreme Court (Nigeria)
CEO, Complete Legal Solutions
CEO, Akindele, Segun & Associates
President, Mountain Man Enterprises
Director, Newsstand Agencies Ltd.
President, THE AKINDELE FOUNDATION (NGO)
Chairman, HTC
Editor, DEMOKRAZYONLINE.COM
Publisher, COMMUNITY ADVOCATE (Free Legal updates)
President, PPDS
Former Director of Litigation, WCNLS
Former Editor in chief of THE AFRICAN TORCH
Former Deputy Director, Court Consent Decrees Implementation Team
Former Spokesperson for Justice and Democracy Advocacy Group
Former President, Oak Group Investment, Inc.
Former Director, Oak Group (non-profit) Inc. (NGO)
Author of several Published Books and dozens of Articles
TV, Radio & Newspaper contributor

Motivational Speaker
Advocate and Legal Counsel for Children & indigent families
Life Coach
Mentor
Poet **& former candidate for elective office**

—ww◦c━▶◦━⊶◦ww—

A FESTERING SORE . . .

—ww◦c━▶◦━⊶◦ww—

Prior to the 1960 independence of Nigeria from British colonial rule, declassified accounts indicate that the British manipulated the national census to favor the North. It also helped to rig (Tafa Balewa's) NPC into office, and talked the late Zik (and the NCNC) into serving as the ceremonial President (and the junior partner in a government of 'national unity') rather than form a coalition with Awolowo of the Action Group.

So, clearly, we started on a very flawed foundation and the seeds of discord and internal divisions were effectively planted to ensure that as long as we remained divided, the British (and other outside interests) would always indirectly call the shots (even as we deluded ourselves about being a truly independent nation).

The above, including personal ambition, unwarranted suspicion, arrogance, self-delusion and a number of other factors led to a series of other events that cascaded out of control, including the incarceration of Awolowo (not unconnected to his rivalry with the Akintola faction in the West), the 1966 coup, the assassination of Ironsi and Fajuyi (plus a number of easterners doing business in the north), the ascension of Gowon (first to accomplish an ill-considered northern secession agenda, and then with the instigation of the British, a timely reversal, especially given the rich oil fields in the Midwest and the Eastern Region of the country) and ultimately (Ojukwu's calculated analysis and) the eventual civil war causing the untimely and unnecessary death of at least a million citizens (mostly in the east).

In 1979, we had the ineffectual NPN regime foisted on the nation by Obsanjo and the military oligarchy looking to protect its flanks with successors who (unlike the sometimes impolitic Awolowo) were less interested in administrative investigations and probes designed to hold them accountable for years of misrule and graft.

In 1993, acting with impunity, Babangida and members of his ilk talked themselves into cancelling the June 12 elections, despite the fact that it was probably the freest and fairest elections ever conducted in the country's history.

In 1998, Abdulsalam Abubakar's regime (upon replacing the fearsomely medieval Abacha regime) began and ultimately succeeded in undermining the national momentum for a new beginning by working to foist Obasanjo, one of its own (and a member of the discredited military oligarchy) on the country; a barely disguised strategy to tamp down the momentum for a thorough house cleaning, thereby buying critical time for the ruling oligarchy to reorganize and ultimately re-assert itself.

In 1999, Buhari, Babangida and Abdulsalam (three former heads of state still collecting pension paid from the nation's resources) openly placed themselves above the law when they declined the (morally binding) summons to appear and give testimony before the Oputa Panel that was set up to get to the bottom of a number of vexing national matters which to this day continue to be unresolved, constituting a potential gathering storm over the national polity.

Beginning in 1999, the corrupt (scattered across virtually all the then existing political parties) were freely unleashed on the political landscape. It became common place for members of the executive and the legislative branch across the country to get caught up in one corruption scandal or another.

Yet somehow, the system was so accommodating of these unseemly practices that most of the perpetrators got away unscathed. And the few that the media identified only suffered momentary embarrassments as they were promptly accorded A SOFT LANDING by the permissive culture in place.

In 2003, Obasanjo's PDP engineered one of the most embarrassing electoral farces in the history of the country.

But they found a way to top even that with the 2007 electoral debacle!

And so we move even that much closer to the very edge of the precipice.

Democracy cannot long survive without a viable and credible opposition. Perhaps that is the objective.

The current oligarchy continues to feign commitment to a constitutional representative government while systematically decimating any form of opposing views; muscling the nation toward an imposed one-party state (in the name of peace and stability), notwithstanding the consequence to our national cohesion, sense of participation and ultimate collective growth.

The only way forward is to arrive at a point where citizens are permitted (after an appropriate national dialogue of whatever name, shape or form) to effectively formalize and put in place institutions that will achieve the same type of salutary vision eloquently articulated by the United States Continental Congress of July 4, 1776 by resolving on our behalf that;

"We (too) hold these truths to be self-evident;
That all men (and women) are created equal;
That they are endowed by their creator with certain inalienable rights;
That among these is life, liberty and the pursuit of happiness;
That to secure these rights;
Governments are instituted among men;
Deriving their just powers from the consent of the governed;
That whenever any form of government becomes destructive to these ends;
It is the right of the people to alter or to abolish it;
And to institute new government;
Laying the foundation on such forms
As to them shall seem most likely to effect their safety and happiness"

THE ABOVE APPROACH WILL USHER IN A NEW AGE OF REASON.

The alternative is to continue on our currently doomed course which is reminiscent of the type of chaotic society envisioned in Thomas Hobbes' Leviathan where FORCE (AND A STATE OF WAR) IS THE ORDER OF THE DAY; AN ENVIRONMENT WHERE LIFE FOR MANY PEOPLE IS NASTY, BRUTISH AND SHORT. Sound familiar?

We have the ability to revert course. We are not destined or wedded to this failed course. We have to breathe life into a locally fashioned form of representative government.

We have to strengthen the judiciary, reform the military and other paramilitary forces like the police, institute comprehensive electoral and campaign finance reforms, eliminate current rules granting outrageous immunity to elected officials, sharpen the independence and creative tension between the executive, judiciary and the legislative branch, ensure a responsible but unfettered and independent media (as a viable fourth estate) and conduct a more comprehensive and robust review of all the other national institutions (including the bureaucracy) that help sustain a thriving socio-economic and political milieu for all citizens.

When something is not working optimally, it makes sense to review and revise it in order to achieve the desired outcomes.

For example, the current mentality across all the states and local government headquarters is all about GETTING, SPENDING AND WAITING AGAIN FOR THE NEXT FEDERAL ALLOCATION.

This is ridiculous. This CENTRAL CONTROL approach to governance has fostered corruption, inhibited local accountability, dampened regional creativity (especially with respect to alternative sources of resource generation).

True federalism, for example has the potential of ginning up local creativity and sense of ownership for the unique approaches crafted to address uniquely regional issues, as opposed to the one-size fits all mentality of the unitary form of government imposed over the years by the military.

How could you accomplish national growth without appropriate national planning? How could you intelligently, equitably and patriotically plan without adequate and accurate information (like an ACCURATE CENSUS untainted by local politics and frivolous ethnic rivalries)?

"IF I WERE A POET"
Am I required to think
that poetry is totally inspired?
That it flows, if at all
instinctively and with great gust
without any conscious effort
to tailor the thoughts
and fashion the language?
Am I to await that faithful gust
and unconscious eloquence
to sort through and express
these seemingly convoluted thoughts
that keep humming in my head
and the tuneless verses of music
still dancing in my soul?
Should I hope that this faithful gust
of inspired intuition and wisdom
will not knock on my door at night
when fatigue has set in and my eyes are closed
when my hands are asleep
and my mind, locked in an erotic dream
awash in unspoken poetry, still?
But why free up a stated hour
if it is indeed as reputed
such a forceful gust
of unconscious eloquence
then I might well be knocked cold
in drunken stupor
still, this force should cobble together
with dexterity and ease
those magical rhymes
even from the cluttered state
of my disheveled mind
(AOA)

In the inspiring tradition of great poets like Chinua Achebe and Wole Soyinka, Attorney Akindele (in recognition of our interrelated destiny) has endeavored to employ poetry to inspire and challenge the next generation of Africans, African Americans and others around the world.

Dr. Akindele with Professor Wole Soyinka conferring during a pro-democracy event organized by the USA based Nigerian Forum for Democracy (NIFOD) for which Akindele was a key spokesperson.

NIFOD collaborated with other major organizations and credible individuals to fight for the installation of democracy in Nigeria.

The current 'demo-krazy' foisted on the nation (by the military oligarchy) would be laughable if it were not such a tragic turn for the country and many of us who sacrificed so much for the installation of a truly representative government that would be guided by the rule of law and thus accountable to the people. Well, for us and especially the next generation, the struggle certainly continues . . .

The assaulted 'Truth' we bore witness to in (my first Book) THE MILITARY FRANCHISE still stares us in the face un-redressed well over a decade later

Barrister Akindele addressing attendees and the media during the 1994 Book dedication event for THE MILITARY FRANCHISE (one of the attendees was a former Federal Minister and Journalist, Prince Tony Momoh, seen here sitting to the left of Barrister Akindele)

Akindele at a press conference with members of the media discussing issues and his vision for a free and democratic society administered by inspired public servants guided by the rule of law

Societies that fail to learn from their sordid pasts are, like infantile tyros, liable to replicate (even celebrate as norm) what in fact should give them pause!

Dr. Akin O. Akindele and his family in the USA

. . . TO WHOM MUCH IS GIVEN, MUCH IS EXPECTED

PROLOGUE

Many wonder WHY SO MUCH OF AFRICA'S TREMENDOUS POTENTIAL, its vast resources, INCLUDING ITS HUMAN CAPITAL go to waste as the Continent continues to fall well short of its great promise.

The following pages (as a follow up to THE MILITARY FRANCHISE and PEOPLE, PASSION, PURPOSE) will articulate some of those reasons.

More importantly, these pages will reveal (and also reiterate some of) the credible routes for ultimate success.

I believe it was Albert Einstein who famously noted that doing the same thing over and over and expecting a different result is tantamount to craziness. Actually, I call it foolishness

Amorphous still
Like the shapes
Of our lives
With elbows bruised
And failing knees
That once ached
With every thrust
Until we reach
The breaking point
That eases the pain
Of the flesh
With pinched nerves
Transplanted
From our once

Steely resolve
And tireless drive
And soon
Meekly
We too would amble
Down the pathways
To our new resting place
So as to make room
For others
Who, acting like fools
Might blindly
Follow our lead

NOW IF NIGERIA (AND INDEED AFRICA) DESIRES TO AVOID
RUNNING IN CIRCLES AS IT'S DONE RATHER INEFFECTUALLY
OVER THE PAST SEVERAL DECADES, THEN IT MUST HEED THE
POPULAR ADMONISHMENT WHICH REMINDS US THAT;

> **"The best way to predict the (preferred salutary) future is to
> Create it"**

Otherwise, we will remain stuck in managed mediocrity. Indeed after many
wasted years and missed opportunities at greatness, most of the citizens of
Africa are properly nonplussed.

Filled with consternation at their socio-political and economic circumstances,
Nigerians, certainly, and indeed most African countries are sadly trapped
in a revolving state of PURGATORY and the buffeted citizens forced to
respectively cogitate with genuine obfuscation as follows;

How did it come to this?
Why are we in this place?
Chilled with desolation
The darkness is thick with uncertainty
The weight of this eerie fog exhausts
Even as one strives to exult

Are we here to be cleansed?
Of all that shackles and ails our spirit
Are we to be teased and challenged

By life's convoluted intrigues
Or are we indeed here to be submerged
And to be sunk in the very depths of ominous despair

Are we destined in time to partake of life's exhilaration?
And to soar with the thrill that attends inevitable reprieve
Are we here to, in time behold and bask
In the majesty of the rainbow
As it hatches even from the womb of human despair
To glorify the heavens and illuminate troubled souls?

How did it come to this?
Why are we in this place?
This desolate milieu for those that crave hope
This leveling desert for those thirsting for a leg up
Alas, are we perchance here to be one of these lost souls
That have been consigned to call this chilling place home?
How did it come to this?
Pray tell, why are we in this place?

This is the misery of Africa and the so-called third world. If the truth be told (apart of South Africa's and perhaps Ghana's modest political advances in recent years), there is currently no single country (or for that matter no single city in America (including DETROIT, MICHIGAN) under the control of a majority African (black) population and African (black) leadership that is satisfactorily meeting its potential, much less thriving!!!

HOPEFULLY, OBAMA'S ASCENSION WILL BEGIN TO CHANGE THAT EQUATION (AT LEAST IN THE CONTEXT OF AFRICAN AMERICANS IN THE UNITED STATES).

Of course, there are examples of under-performance in some communities involving other races too.

But it is especially poignant and galling that Africans cannot honestly point to a country and take pride in the CURRENT accomplishments of its leadership.

This is true about the grossly under performing Nigeria, South Africa, and Egypt, all of whom should be the three main socio-economic pillars of Africa.

So it becomes necessary to ask; WHY

Why does fate bless some
With abundance and beauty
And leave others bereft of hope and appeal
Yet, like the reddish Rose that flowers with appeal
Even the blessed are cursed with thorns in their beauty
Oh dear world, not so rounded, not so perfect and wholesome

Why do birds choose to sing
To delight tone-deaf trees
And the ugly larvae grows to become a beautiful butterfly
Only to glorify arid seasons and feast on lowly flies
Yet, many dynamic souls are grounded to the earth like trees
Unable to soar with the birds that sing

Why spend an eon laboring to mount the crest
Only to get to the summit and be challenged by the next
And in a whimsical moment tear to shreds
What was carefully woven with iron threads?
Belatedly, we make the best quest of life the next
Even as the zeal to surmount the rest begins to crest

Why?

To paraphrase Shakespeare, the problem may well not be in our stars or some cosmic misfortune or circumstance for which we are thoroughly blameless and without some measure of control.

Come on, let's be honest with ourselves. THE ROAD TRAVELED thus far has been substantially of our own making.

In Nigeria, for example, we had (and still have many) thoroughly inspiring (though imperfect) trail blazing giants. We've been blessed with leaders like Obafemi Awolowo, Herbert Macaulay, Nnamdi Azikiwe, Anthony Enahoro and Aminu Kano (among others).

Additional, the next generation of leaders that came after them gave us inspiring figures that included Professor Ayodele Awojobi, Gani Fawehinmi, Wole Soyinka, Balarabe Musa, Beko Ransome Kuti, Fela Anikulapo Kuti

and (later in his life) the somewhat taciturn General Tunde Idiagbon (of the War Against Indiscipline (WAI) fame).

Each of these people spoke to us eloquently both in their verbal communications, but most importantly with the profound choices they made as clear examples to the rest of us.

The surest way out of the travails afflicting Nigeria and much of Africa is to humbly concede that these leaders were right. We must, like the prodigal son, take stock and timely change our ways.

We must unabashedly adopt much of the wisdom behind the socio-economic and political compass they each spent a lifetime helping to articulate or fashion out of love for their fellow men and inspired by the sheer audacity of their inclusive vision about our collective humanity.

While many current leaders have elected political corruption and a self-serving agenda, it would have been easy to stay the course and keep Africa's feet firmly planted on the progressive road that was being blazed for us to travel.

Indeed, unlike the forgettable lives of Abacha, Babangida, Obasanjo and the likes of the Ubas and Nzeribe (men who had it all, yet fumbled everything, even the chance to be truly great), when you think about (any of) the true African heroes like Awolowo, Mandela, Nkrumah and Sankara, the following inspirational lessons come to mind;

Each of these great and inspired lives has been
What we all should aspire to be
Each stood tall and walked the road
His every step heavy as a load
But each of them had firmly placed his feet
On this course for his salutary destiny to meet

You each have had your moments
You even overcame some torments
The vision was blurry from the cloud
But your focus was sharp there is no doubt

The lesson of your life
Is simple and clear

It says follow your mind
Not merely your kind
Let your genius flow
Don't merely go
With the flow
If you truly want to grow

It has been quite inspiring
Reflecting back on how each of you traveled this road

The many temptations on the path of progressive forces are legion. It is critical to avoid winning the corrupted moment at the expense of losing the winnable season!

To that end, we must exhort current and future leaders to be wary of the **TEMPTING ROAD BEST LEFT UNTRAVELED**. AFTERALL, THERE IS VALUE IN STAYING THE COURSE ON THE MATCH TOWARD JUSTICE AND A LIFE OF INTEGRITY.

Temptation to falter is a normal part of this journey. For me at least, and certainly for most Africans DREAMING OF, HOPING FOR AND INSISTING UPON a better life and viable Nation States they could proudly call their own, the primary objective offers much more than the temporal gains available to those who choose to falter and prematurely cry uncle.

Yes
It was awhile back
Now that I look back
When the fork crossed my path
The season my doubts and I had to part

At that fateful junction of life
When doubt and vision dueled for life
I chose the course that gave me HOPE
The lighted path of wisdom, lest I grope

Even as I stumble and fall
Through the dark valleys and the abyss of my call
I rise and rise again to stay the course
My shoulders are straight, my back is tall, and I am on course

As I confront the final treachery of the abyss
That painted altar glistened temptingly anew to appease
Tired legs in the wake of the steepest climb
Yet I stayed the course
And now I am on course
For glory waits at the crest of my climb

BEFORE WE PROCEED FURTHER, FIRST A PRELIMINARY COGITATION CONCERNING SOME PHILOSOPHICAL MUDDY WATERS

In the context of whether to keep hope alive or to falter;

Some may well ask
How universal is a particular notion of goodness
How enduring through the generations
Are the current conceptions of what is good or evil
How fleeting, indeed how checkered
Are the fortunes of currently
Exulted attributes
How obdurate and impervious to malice
And condemnation are the conducts and tendencies
We currently loath and consign as mean
Is goodness good for all seasons
Is a current evil cursed
With an intrinsic defect
Do we celebrate goodness for its sake
Or do we align with our version of it
As it tends to serve our purpose
Do we merely despise and rebuke a conduct
Because it is the season to do so

Or are we compelled to be so disposed
Even when the season is less reproachful
And our interests and happiness beg for its exultation
If real happiness is being true to ourselves
And our desires
Shouldn't goodness and evil be thus exorcised
Of all intrinsic values
And be saddled only with attributes
That our current hopes and desires
Require us to adorn on them
Indeed, where does evil lurk
Is it in the tortured minds
Of treacherous men
Who contrive them
Or is it as nebulous and ephemeral
Even as the wind blows
By retail from different sides
To appease changing seasons

FREE YOUR IMAGINATIVE FANCY AND
LET GO OF YOUR FEARS!

While we are at it, **a few words on courage and convictions**. After all, it is strength (of character) that makes other virtues possible.

The **future development of Africa is not going to be solely dependent on its leadership, but more so, on its people.**

It will depend on their desire and conscious insistence on justice and the rule of law. A lot will depend on their perseverance and doggedness.

To that end, each citizen is responsible for their effective or ineffectual political activism or social apathy.

The only way forward is for every person of conscience to take a stand and act on their respective convictions!

Because,
Beyond this place
Of toothless gab
And mere pontification
Is a region of realism
And circumstance
Where people must free themselves
From their own
Self-imposed edict
Of limited thought and contemplation
It is appropriate
That people reflect
And analyze what afflicts them
Without glorifying it
By sheer puzzlement of countenance
And continued inaction
To rectify the very sorry nature
Of their station

After all, if indeed we have some fundamental rights, the ability to think freely should be one of them.

Abolition or unjustifiable abridgement of this essential freedom of expression, belief or association is arguably equivalent to a living death. For then, you would merely be 'existing' and not really living and flourishing.

I call this a (curable) state of ANNA MARIE'S BLUES.

AFRICANS MUST UNLEASH THEIR POTENTIAL BY LIBERATING THEMSELVES FROM THE TYRANNY OF THE PUPPETMASTERS.

THEY MUST DEFY THOSE WHO PUT DUBIOUS LIMITS ON THEIR FREEDOM OF EXPRESSION, BELIEF, ASSOCIATION AND ESSENTIAL HUMANITY.

LIKE THE IDEALIZED 'ANNA MARIE' OF MY IMAGINATIVE
FANCY, EACH MUST BREAK FREE OF THIS INHIBITING
PSYCHOLOGICAL CHAIN, SO THAT OSTENSIBLY FREE CITIZENS
ARE ULTIMATELY . . .

No longer playing
Or praying
By the rules imposed
To depose
Natural instincts
And desires to be distinct
The rules imposed by fools
And cynically handed down
By clowns
In crowns
And gowns
Intending to define
And commanding we not defy
Subjective constructs
They construct
To control
And patrol
Even discreet thoughts
That don't amount to Torts
We seek the joys others define
And leave unattended
The essential cravings of our soul
As we strive vainly to please others
With silly appearances that are mostly self imposed
Happiness deferred
Ultimately, is happiness denied!

IF I WERE AN INSPIRATIONAL POET

Would I still be required to think
That poetry flows like inebriating drink
The moment you permit your mind or finger
To purposefully linger

On any chatter
That may matter
To the budding poet
Reckoning to make a point?

Should I still hope
That rather than grope
For phrases to rhyme
For little children to mime
I may very well be knocked cold
And too much in a drunken stupor to take hold
Of my conscious senses, yet those magical and inspirational rhymes
Will still be cobbled together for little children to mime?

How inspired must I be
Perhaps like the tenacious and purposeful little Bee
What initial price must I pay
Hopefully, no more than the penitent kneeling to pray
Yet this humble drunken fool's bold
Reward he views as gold
May yet be mined
From a humble mind
That purposefully folds
Magically inspirational words
On immortal tablets to be told
Through songs for miming little children
Before they are too old
To be captivated
By the magical rhymes that need to take hold

So I mime
The rhymes
To the sensational
And the inspirational
Chatters
That hopefully matter
Even as I grope
In hope
For subjective acclaim

So I may lay claim
And be acknowledged finally
And eternally
To be that tenaciously inspirational poet
That succeeded in finally making his inspired point

(About the ardently unshakeable urgency for positive change)

Now, **IF YOU WERE AN ISPIRATIONAL POET-YOU** would use words to inspire millions to do the right thing by their fellow men.

However, **YOU** don't have to be a Poet to motivate and lead with **YOUR ACTIONS.**

PURPOSEFUL ACTION BY EACH OF US WILL SPEAK LOUDER AND MORE ELOQUENTLY THAN MERE WORDS!

Words without follow up actions are no more impressive than a showering inferno of towering snow flakes falling lamely and without pageantry on an impervious concrete slab!!!

For many people in Africa, it has been a bitter legacy of hard life, learning to deal with hard knocks and sentenced to cope with nothing more than a cycle of hard times.

There comes a time in the life of a community when every man and woman of conscience is invited to keep an appointed date with destiny. These are times when new leaders are weaned, future legends made, when the young come of age and the rites of passage are complete.

For much of Africa, and certainly for those in Nigeria, the time for meaningful action and **CHANGE** is long over due.

Without further delay, we must begin to insist on freely and fairly choosing our leaders. We must begin to insist on making them accountable to our needs.

We all have an obligation to care and to remain somehow engaged in the political process. FAILURE IS NOT AN OPTION. Failure to embrace and surmount this challenge will ultimately cede political power and the ability to effect meaningful change to those who could care less about a progressive agenda of elevating political justice, social equity, economic fairness and the rule of law.

The level of engagement for some may well not exceed exercising the right to vote on election-day, while remaining vigilant that the overall electoral process is substantially fair (even if not perfectly so).

If enough people in any society invest in this minimum level of engagement, I dare say that the political community in question will, over time, begin to see its will reflected in those who ultimately get elected and in the policies and programs accorded priority in the political discourse.

Soon enough, water scarcity, epileptic electricity, massive food shortages and unaffordable housing will be a thing of the past. But only if more of us get actively involved in DEMANDING OUR RIGHTS!

Whether or not you or I decide to directly participate in PARTISAN POLITICS, we nevertheless have the obligation (like everyone else in society) to insist that those who ascend to political power achieve it fairly (not forcibly or corruptly) and that they do exercise that temporal authority justly, humbly and on behalf of the people.

Everyone, including some of my "progressive" friends (and a few who like to be identified as "important social critics") cannot leave this task to others.

None of us has the luxury of standing aloof, on the sidelines, or worse, losing our nerve by settling for mediocrity in a transparent attempt to win the marginal moment while ultimately losing the winnable season.

For example, a number of my extended family members who should know better (including some previously admired or respected media types and other pro-democracy movement colleagues of bygone years) failed themselves, their conscience and the country during the 2007 electoral farce in Nigeria.

Rather than intelligently "discriminate" with respect to whom to support for particular contested positions irrespective of Political Party affiliation, it was embarrassing to witness otherwise intelligent and ostensibly well-meaning "progressives" not only support (at best) questionable candidates for various offices (including the Presidency and the Governorship positions), but also supporting all the clearly unqualified, incompetent or brazenly corrupt lower ballot candidates hoping to ride the same Political Party coattails.

Yet folks wonder why nothing eventually gets done to improve the people's lives once the "campaign" season is over.

Nobody asks how and why a sitting governor would pretty much get away with using State resources (sometimes in excess of hundreds of millions of Dollars) to buy electoral success rather than employ those resources (as required by law) to enhance the lives of the people.

The reasons are easy to deduce. There is no accountability (other than the few and rather selective embarrassment of political opponents with well orchestrated indictments).

Also noteworthy is the sad reality of disengaged, unmotivated, cynical and previously **disappointed electorates many of whom have been deluded or consciously conscripted with the fallacious notion that in fact you could never "beat them" so you might as well "join them"**

I dare anyone to point to any meaningful progress (or some legitimate 'dividends of democracy') they have enjoyed that could justify the BILLIONS IN DOLLARS BUDGETED AND UNACCOUNTED FOR OVER THE PAST DECADE OR SO!

How intelligent is it for people to settle for a few crumbs doled out to buy their support (and to shut them up for the next four to eight years) while the 'elected' official openly and with impunity lines his or her pocket, living large and in obscene opulence while the population is barely able to eke out its daily bread.

Now, how outrageously offensive is that? Anyone that does not find this kind of outcomes unacceptable and unedifying is either mentally ill-clad or too cynical and corrupt to be allowed near the electoral process (much less be permitted to run it).

Partly buoyed by ambition and possibly a desire to do some good (if doable), one witnessed otherwise decent folks get entangled in the political process.

Unfortunately, by allowing others (sometime referred to as Political godfathers) to pay (or supplement) their way into office, they become permanently beholden to the pied Piper that ultimately dictates the political tune they are allowed to play.

Folks who so easily discard their values and the salutary objective behind their original involvement in partisan politics are probably better off not to have joined in the first place.

Because, not only will they not accomplish the salutary goals (having readily traded their political souls to the local political godfather), but more often than not, the material rewards they get in return are ultimately not as enduring as what they frivolously traded away for the (Judas-Iscariot) thirty bloody pieces of silver.

This is often the **danger of blindly joining** any so-called 'established or winning party.' Unless you're cynically willing to suspend disbelief in the banal and empty rhetoric being peddled by a cabal you know deep down is only interested in power, solely for its selfish ends.

ANYBODY IS FREE TO JOIN ANY PARTY AS LONG AS THE MOTIVATION IS HONEST PUBLIC SERVICE, RATHER THAN A CYNICAL SHORT CUT FOR PERSONAL AGGRANDISEMENT

Which is why (**except in very few instances**), the refrain that the so-called reputed progressive joined a questionable group so as to make **"changes from within"** sound so hollow, because judgment is made, not by anybody's rhetoric, but by the unequivocal actions and choices they make when the going gets tough!

Now, we are the outcomes of all our life's experiences. Hence we will not all see things the same way. This is why some people may be more liberal than others on particular issues and while some may be more conservative than others on a variety of other issues.

Legitimate differences of opinion are healthy in any progressing and free society. It ought to be celebrated and openly debated rather than demonized even in a partisan political contest.

Bottom line, I believe in politics without rancor or bitterness. As long as the differences are borne of honestly held ideas and opinion, as opposed to a cynical attempt to oppress, to corrupt or to set society back in a self-serving attempt at personal or group aggrandizement or subjugation.

That is where I come down and hence the visionary predicate to how I see Africa's political future evolve . . .

BOOK
CHAPTERS

1.

A WAKE UP CALL TO THE
(SO-CALLED) 'PROGRESSIVES'

There are many reasons why the United States became the greatest country in the world. There was a reason why the United Kingdom (particularly the England, despite being a relatively tiny country) was able to dominate the world for a while during the heights of the British Empire. Riding American coattails in recent years (even into George Bush's Iraq misadventure), it has remained doggedly involved in all the major issues of concern around the world. The following therefore bears repeating.

Americans are not from Mars. Britons were not descended from Venus. These societies were blessed with leaders with great visions who saw and seized the opportunity for greatness and international accomplishments for their respective societies.

In the early 1960s, India, Brazil and Nigeria were identified by the United Nations as the next set of emerging nations likely to become industrialized and potentially great.

Well, India and Brazil (and now China) have met that target and in some respects exceeded the projections.

Meanwhile Nigeria has markedly regressed with the succession of greedy, unimaginative and mentally ill-clad leaders and a people whose self-confidence has been shaken (rather than stirred toward greater ideals and accomplishments).

It's time to take stock (and be honest with ourselves) even as we strive for a new re-awakening!

As the saying goes, the best way to predict the future is to create it. And in that regard, instead of being wishy-washy and ineffectual about what was and what could have been, intelligently addressing the current unacceptable reality should be the focus.

The PRESENT is what you deal with.
The PAST is gone
And done
With

The only value of reflecting on the past is to help focus the mind on the constructive lessons learned along the way.

While we may have no control over the circumstances surrounding the times in which we live, we certainly can control what we make of the circumstances we find ourselves.

To that end, if we truly desire SOCIO-POLITICAL JUSTICE AND A SOCIETY THAT ALLOWS US TO THRIVE AND TO FREELY PURSUE OUR RESPECTIVE SOURCES OF HAPPINESS, we must persevere while allowing ourselves to be inspired by the types of creative and profoundly great and life altering examples referenced in this and related books.

We must reflect and explore a different approach in this quest. This is because, even though we **(the so-called 'Progressives' and pro-democracy advocates) generally mean well for our respective communities, we** are often overly cerebral and philosophical while forgetting to be sufficiently pragmatic in our quest for the ultimate results we seek.

Consistently (in the long-joined dialectic battle for the soul and ultimate advancement of Nigeria, Nay Africa), we've been defeated by the more practical men who know how to corruptly seize, cynically wield and brutally retain power at any cost.

They've been doing it successfully since the early 1960s. Aside from a few instances of calculated retreats, they've generally worsted us in

this quest for ascendancy. Hence the long stalled socio-economic and political development of Africa.

To forestall this from happening again in the 2007 elections, I made concerted efforts to reach out to and warn a number of my colleagues in the progressive movement (at least two years ahead of the battle that was inevitably going to be joined).

Unfortunately, some were blinded by ego, some by anger, a few, understandably by fatigue and others by their naiveté or other distractions.

The bottom line was that not enough of them were listening or willing to timely heed my (or other similar) call for a UNITED FRONT!!!

Let us reflect on our missed opportunities and learn from them going forward.

WE SHOULDN'T MERELY SECRETLY LONG FOR BETTER DAYS AND FAST FADING DREAMS. WE SHOULD OPENLY EMBRACE THE POSSIBILITIES AND THE LIFE AFFIRMING MESSAGE OF THIS KINDRED SOUL!

MAY DAY! MAY DAY! ANOTHER UNINSPIRED DAY

From Independence DAY; To Election DAY; To FEDECO/ INEC Favorable Result Sale DAY; To June 12 Day; To Demo-Krazy DAY—

Life for most people in Africa has been a succession of grossly uninspired days!

No wonder
The proud Hibiscus
Shrivels and pouts
In the wake
Of a diffuse
And indifferent
Early morning glare
Of a dull autumn day
And with retracted petals
The flowery peacocks
Flop in unison
To rebel
Against the gloom
Of a most
Uninspired day

WITH A PATTERN SO ODIOUS AND UNINSPIRING, ISN'T IT
ABOUT TIME WE DREW A LINE IN THE SAND AND INSISTED
ENOUGH WAS ENOUGH?

Oh, kirikiri, full of gruff and swagger
A foreboding dungeon with steel gates
Tall fences and trigger happy death angels
Standing guard like vultures, waiting to prey

Kirikiri, built as the great social equalizer
Operated instead as a place the rich and powerful
Consign tiresome social commentators
Who decline to take a hint and tore the line

YES, THEY HAVE IMPRISONED THOUSANDS AND KILLED EVEN
MORE. Think about it, FROM IRONSI AND FAJUYI, TO BOLA IGE
AND DELE GIWA, INCLUDING KUDIRAT ABIOLA AND MANY
OTHERS.

THEY'VE DONE THEIR WORSE. WHAT ELSE CAN THEY STEAL?
FOR THAT MATTER WHAT ELSE CAN THEY INFLICT ON US
THAT THEY HAVEN'T ALREADY?

So what do you have to lose by standing up with other progressive forces to insist on your rights and dignity?

The only thing you're likely to achieve by keeping quiet and accepting all the oppression and socio-political disregard for your interests (or for that matter, joining the perpetrators of the oppression because you cannot see your way clear of defeating them) is to possibly grow old and die quietly after an unimpressive life **(assuming you escape an untimely death from armed robbers made more numerous by the unjust system, water pollution, lack of appropriate or timely medical services, a possible gruesome demise from the many ill-maintained roads . . . SHOULD I GO ON?).**

So, the choice is yours. But what a waste that would be, should you elect to live like an INTELLECTUAL AND EMOTIONAL ZOMBIE.

A QUICK SLAP DOWN TO THE DISENGAGED AND SOCIALLY ALOOF NON-VOTING 'INTELLECTUAL'

It is often amusing to hear some otherwise smart folks suggest that all they care about is focusing only on themselves, their jobs and their family and all will be well. Balderdash!

Will they not ply the same inaccessible roads to their job locations? Will they and their families' welfare and general safety not be equally threatened by hoodlums and collaborating policemen who control our streets?

Do they think that they are better off merely erecting taller fences for their homes instead of us insisting together on better law enforcement for our collective security?

Perhaps some of these folks are not that smart after all. Perhaps some of these folks are just too selfish to see beyond their compromised noses. **Yes, they somehow managed to secure some material comforts. Now, they mean to quietly enjoy it without being distracted by all the mayhem and social upheaval around them. Good luck!**

Actually, a few of them somehow pull it off. But for many of these types of self-absorbed uppity folks, sooner or later, they get ensnared by the social monster they hoped to avoid and could have helped contain before it became too formidable to easily manage.

Now, despite precariously straddling the 'upper middle class status' in A COUTRY OF THE BLIND (given that this is a society that is substantially lawless), from time to time, these types of folks get their comeuppance. Sometimes by the rude and crude police corporal who (in exchange for monetary delivery to his bosses at the station), is a law unto himself at his illegally erected police check point (or toll gate, if we are to be more accurate).

Sooner or later they too will fall victim to this extortion scheme disguised as some legitimate exercise of verifying some mythical vehicle 'particulars' while looking longingly and with greed at their life of opulence or the occasional tubers of yam stored in the trunk of their imported vehicles.

Or when they have to swat at mosquitoes all night in the dark because, as usual, NEPA (or Power Holding) has decided to hold on to electric supplies for the next three weeks, and due to poor government policies that they've never concerned themselves with, our national refineries are moribund, so even though we have some of the best crude oil and gas supplies in the world, we actually have to import them refined at higher prices and consequently, there is always a shortfall and long queues at petrol stations.

And from time to time, there just isn't any readily available to fill and sustain the noisy generators of the rich and well connected for its nightly run.

So, on such 'rare' occasions, these folks get to swat at mosquitoes all night. Well, this is just another brief moment in time highlighting the inter-connected nature of our national destiny.

WELCOME BACK TO THE REAL WORLD, CHIEF, DOCTOR, ALHAJI, PASTOR, MR 'DISCONNECTED INTELLECTUAL'

A CAUTIONARY NOTE TO THE UP AND COMING
MR & MRS 'WISE-MAN'

Ah!

That enchanted season

Too fleeting but divine

The ghosts of desks bunched up

And chalks and scattered thoughts

The clear faces and the bones of dead memories rise unleashed to mock this day.

Vibrant blessings that once begged for attention presently elude the grasp of our aging bones but stoically, we reminisce

And we smile wanly and with sad eyes

As we confront the giggling parody of our early years. We that once terrorized the school hall ways the lunch rooms and the girls' lavatories are now being led gingerly

Across vacated by-ways

Guided through cloak rooms, prune rooms and revolving laboratories

Even by the youths unleashed

To remind us of our diminished strength as we are ferried through graying avenues

That once celebrated our vibrant energy and youth.

Ah!

Those bunched up desks,

Those chalks and scattered thoughts

How did it all come to this?

Our early strength deluded us about our limitations. And our exuberance clouded our vision.

Now, with the wisdom of the years,

How easy would it now be to actually move the move-able

And to conserve the youthful vitality

That once was wasted on futile and quixotic angry whacks at bodies immovable that merely remained unimpressed even as we waxed philosophical in futile rage.

Ah!

That enchanted season

Truly divine but fleeting

If only we were blessed with new vitality

To appease these restless minds

And give these tired bones timely solace

From their progressive atrophy, and

From tiresome memories of promises unfulfilled

Which flash intermittently with bright images that tease and from these old
creaking desks, the messy chalks and those scattered thoughts . . .
Who did you say you were again, son?

MR WISE-MAN, I SUPPOSE?

INEBRIATING DRUGS AS A METAPHOR FOR THE CORRUPTING CULTURE OF 'POLITICAL SETTLEMENT' IN AFRICA!

Political sell-outs are morally not much better than low-life cocaine or crack
dealers. So take heed and stay smart.

Stay smart
Don't start
Or get hooked on drugs
It will clog
And in time weaken
Your heart from ticking

Stay smart
Don't snack
On a pack
Of crack
It soils and powders your nose
And strangles your hopes and dreams like a noose

Stay smart
Don't start
To snack
On a pack

Of crack
Be smart

**In reality, being afraid of asserting your right does not mean you'll
be spared the death (or oppression) you are so afraid of which causes
you to vacillate and remain physically immobilized, and intellectually
paralyzed.**

Alas
We leave unattended
The needs to be tended
As we search and row
For a blissful tomorrow

But all our yesterdays
Are gone forever
And not a single tomorrow
Is assured

So, live a little less
For a better tomorrow
And live a little more today
Dwell a little less
On a happier tomorrow
And make your happiest day today

**IN THE SPIRIT OF LIVING A LITTLE, I WOULD LIKE TO
CHALLENGE YOU POLITICAL NEOPHYTES OUT THERE TO
SOW YOUR POLITICAL WILD OATS BEFORE YOU'RE TOAST!**

Sow your wild oats
Before you're toast
Bake your own roast
Before you're trapped by a silly 'GODFATHER'S' boast

Silky negligee
Tossed carelessly on your nestling blue jay
Lacy racy underwear
You hope one day to wear

The feel of ELECTORAL satin sheets
As you snuggle contentedly beneath the sheets
With a well perfumed POLITICAL Ballerina
Performing at this discreet arena
And the careless horny fool is toast
Doomed perhaps by his boast
Even before he is ready to coast
For life without parole
In domesticated dungeon with a designing POLITICAL host

Sow your wild oats
Before you're toast
Bake your own roast
Before you're trapped FOR LIFE by a silly boast

The instinctive hunter is hunted
And neutered
UNLAWFULLY
But effectively and forcefully
By the obligations of contrived POLITICAL matrimony
Even at the heights of its very disharmony
As the Ballerina's magical perfume loses its charm
And the image conjured by the silk and the lace
Only does your spirit harm
So again I urge you, sow your wild oats
Before you're toast
Bake your own PHILOSOPHICAL roast
Before you're trapped by a TRICKY PARTY and a boast

As I noted earlier, Albert Einstein was correct when he noted that doing the same thing over and over and expecting a different result is tantamount to craziness. Something the irrepressible Fela Anikulapo Kuti would have labeled "FOLLOW-FOLLOW"

Amorphous still
Like the shapes
Of our lives
With elbows bruised
And failing knees
That once ached

With every thrust
Until we reach
The breaking point
That eases the pain
Of the flesh
With pinched nerves
Transplanted
From our once
Steely resolve
And tireless drive
And soon
Meekly
We too would amble
Down the pathways
To our new resting place
So as to make room
For others
Who like fools
Would blindly
Follow our lead

Now, I dream about a time when social amity, political sobriety and economic justice will rule these lands. These are dreams that I cherish. These are dreams I intend to hold on to. These are dreams I plan to give life and turn into reality ANY WAY I CAN! I CANNOT DO THIS BY MYSELF. I NEED THOSE OF YOU WHO SHARE A SIMILAR DREAM TO JOIN IN, TO OPENLY STAND UP AND BE COUNTED. To that end, I humbly commend this salutary dream to each of you. TOGETHER, LET'S CHERISH THIS DREAM! LET'S MAKE IT HAPPEN!!

Cherish your dreams
For without dreams
Life is listless and contained
Like a drifter on a lake

Cherish your dreams
For without dreams
The mind atrophies in moments
And the spirit is without nourishment

Cherish your dreams
For when you dream
Your tremendous promise is unleashed
And your vitality is released

Cherish your dreams
Dream the seemingly impossible dreams
Tame the treachery of the abyss
Redeem your legacy and your piece

Cherish your dreams
Nurture your dreams
Turn them into beacons
A shield against life's sometimes unholy beckons

LET US TURN QUIET DREAMS INTO ACTION PLANS WE PURSUE DURING OUR WAKING MOMENTS!

For far too long, the DESPOTIC African leaders have directly or indirectly forced out many of its best minds and the most able bodied because of oppressive policies that are anathema to any free human spirit.

They call it the CONTINENTAL BRAIN DRAIN. Well, sadly, the casualties of this continental drift are not only those who were left behind to stand up to the foreboding challenges of remorseless tyrants and their agents. The casualties are many. Alas, even the well secured fleeing compatriots (of which I am one) are no less victims of this continental shame.

In a pathetic display of ultimate myopia
We fled abroad in a state of euphoria
Even as we professed
And sometimes promiscuously confessed
Gleefully to be in search of a socio-political Utopia

This utopia continues to prove elusive
Yet, we remain evasive
Both intellectually and in our conduct at the border fences

Stuck in the mirage that plagues our newly contrived defenses
Even as we plot in search of the Prize that remains elusive

Initially, we are filled with vigor in our veins
Even while we searched desperately but in vain
For new roots to sprout and bring forth new life far a-field
On converted cotton fields
With irrigated sweat and blood proceeding forcefully still from tired veins

Sweating up our receding foreheads
Draining away the heat and passion as our subdued heads
Are cooled in places by the waters that lighten
Our weighted wisdom and clouds our once enlightened
Spirit that is now weakened as we redefine our new Utopia

Utopia, the one we came upon in a blinding state of euphoria
A stiff and humbling price for our still uncorrected myopia
And though our frustration may now border on hysteria
Still, the highs though fleeting, were real when we attacked
With gusto, that failed course to momentary utopia
The ones steeped in the mirage of our cluttered consciousness

Yes, we are very much on course
On a bloody brain drain to utopia

"What is a good man but a bad man's teacher? What is a bad man but a good man's job?—Wisdom of the TAO

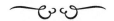

2.

THE GODFATHER GAMBIT

After eight years of fast living, questionable contracts, botched third term power grab, UNRESOLVED ASSASINATIONS (including that of Bola Ige, the then sitting Attorney General), intimidating other opponents and general wanton debauchery, Obasanjo and the now late Adedibu's arrogant surrogates (of AMALA STYLE POLITICS) are now in fast retreat.

Long live the medically hobbled (and thoroughly uninspired) Yar'Ardua and the next group of transitory godfathers!

First they ignore you
Then they laugh at you
Soon after they openly resist and fight you
Eventually they are forced to see the light
And you win!—So goes the saying.

It is therefore no excuse to abandon a just cause merely because it would take some doing and a great deal of overcoming obstacles to achieve.

The saying may now seem trite, but profound nevertheless. Great challenges are nothing more than great opportunities disguised in work clothes.

Further, **difficult challenges we face** from time to time may well be profound. They **do not necessarily build character** (especially when mishandled). **However, they do often REVEAL a person's true character.**

So, before you carelessly and without much reflection mouth that silly refrain that suggests that 'if you cannot beat them, then join them', **take a moment to grow a little backbone and some intestinal fortitude because if the cause you believe in is valuable and worthwhile, it certainly deserves at least your best efforts.**

Yes, at one time or another, we each will be affected by life's sometimes unfair turn of events. But it is totally up to you how you react to life's fortunes and vicissitudes. It will be up to you whether you let temporal set backs or success afflict your spirit and send you into fitful bouts of apoplexy, or whether you will let it infect your sense of proportion and perspective.

Now the following is for those who successfully sell-out and trade their soul to the devil (in particular circumstances), for any temporal gains. Take a moment to ask yourself whether it was worth it. I mean, really worth the trade off. Because in the final analysis, if you gained the "outer world" but can barely look yourself in the mirror then you may have paid too much for your piece of the pie.

You don't want to be a person of apparent success. Your aim is to grow as a person of character, of meaningful convictions and values. Otherwise, your life will degenerate into a meaningless orgy of greed and covert debauchery.

Let me even get a little spiritual here, especially since Africans (and African Americans) are especially religious. The irony has never resolved itself in my mind. How many overtly profess their religious beliefs and yet go out of their way to break many of the most elementary precepts in any religious doctrine merely to keep others down in a cynical effort to attain ultimately meaningless material advantages.

Our talent (or other accidental circumstance) is nature (or God's) gift to enrich our lives and the world in which we live. How we use it is our way of defining our values and sense of perspective and gratitude for our respectively unique opportunity.

Given this predicate, you would understand why many consider political sell-outs morally reprehensible folks afflicted with **political myopia. They choose to lose a winnable war for a brief pyrrhic victory in an ultimately meaningless mini-battle.**

This reminds me of some other misguided compatriots during the height of our struggle for democracy (especially in the USA where I was one of the leading voices).

Sometime between 1994 and 1996 those of us operating in the USA had a series of run-ins with some POLITICAL errand boys (who were merely the paid thugs) of the Abacha terrorist machine.

In response to their attempt to intimidate, infiltrate or corrupt our ranks, I recall sending a clear repelling message their way which resonated clearly.

The message in the following challenge is sadly still relevant TODAY!

June 9, 1994 OPINION
PUBLISHED IN THE TEMPO NEWSPAPER,
"A Word, For Ambassador Kazaure"

Ambassador Kazaure, Nigeria's ambassador to the United States recently circulated a letter specifically targeting pro-democracy organizations in the USA, including the Nigeria Forum for Democracy (NIFOD), and the Democratic Alliance of Nigeria (DAN), urging such—groups to in effect, suspend their activities, and submerge under a front organization called the National Union of Nigerians which is being sponsored by Abacha's military government.

It was quite generous of the Ambassador to now want to unite all Nigerians abroad under this new organization, although we have absolutely no idea how this would facilitate the installment of political democracy and government probity in-our country.

If this effort is to help better coordinate the activities of his office so that services and assistance to Nigerians abroad can be made more efficient, then we would suggest that the real restructuring has to come from the very top, starting with Abacha downwards, including his Excellency, and some of the crooks who work under him.

However, if the motivation behind this effort, as we already suspect, is to silence the stinging voice of opposition abroad, and dilute the effective efforts of pro-democracy forces in the USA, then we can only note that this government's cynicism and disregard for the yearnings of our people is only exceeded by its deviousness and abject myopia

It should read the writing on the wall, in the newspapers, even on people's faces. Enough Is Enough!

The spectacle of a nation like ours,, in spite of our immense human and natural resources remaining no more that, a paper giant; a big for nothing colossus in the middle of an underachieving continent, mired in managed mediocrity by two for a penny dictators is getting to be too much of a painful sight to behold.

What the Abachas; the Shonekans and the Nzeribes of this world should realize is that they may succeed for a while to deny the yearnings of the people with lies, brute force, treachery and intrigue, in time, the people will be pushed to the wall, and a thorough accounting of their stewardship will be required.

No, we regret to announce that we would not be used by the Kazaures of this country for their self-serving agenda.

Instead, we will continue to turn the tables on them and make their unsolicited sojourn at the helm of affairs as unpalatable as they have made the lives of our people wretched and unbearable; turning proud hardworking people into jobless or underemployed beggars and our country a laughing stock around the world.

Make no mistake, despite the obvious treachery of this self-appointed leaders, there are always a few people who either because they are genuinely mistaken, or equally cynical, but nevertheless prepared to prop up these people by serving as their effusive cheerleaders, apologists or die-hard foot soldiers.

Think about it, after all this country had to endure, some people have actually allowed themselves to be quoted as considering Babangida's tenure a blessing for this country, and Abacha's expected ascension to power heralded almost like the much anticipated second coming.

It used to be fashionable for some of us abroad to think that such simpletons and mindless foot soldiers were purely home grown and nurtured in our sheltered climate. Well, we were dead wrong.

Events of recent weeks in the USA which has pitted forces of democratic progress against the paid agents of military domination and other reactionary forces make one reassess prior assumptions. Nigerians (or anyone for that matter) who stand by in silence in the face of tyranny and oppression are equally guilty of complicity by omission and accommodation.

Those who refuse to speak up against injustice are helping to entrench it. Those who refuse to be part of the solution are ultimately part of the problem.

On May first (1994) in Detroit, Michigan, as we were peacefully protesting against the deplorable situation at home (in Nigeria), the unacceptable military rule and official corruption, some favored apologists of the current corrupt system were equally determined to earn their keep by endeavoring to employ brute force to quell our protestations and shield government agents from being presented with a formal (and embarrassing) letter of Protest to Kazaure and his boss at Abuja.

So you see, we in the USA have our own share of "kill and go" (or government paid thugs, for short).

These simple minded thugs fail to realize, that they are mere foot soldiers. We have no quarrel with fellow victimized citizens, even though some may be too blind or stupid to understand that our fight is theirs also; and our success benefits all Nigerians truly seeking justice and fair play.

Our focus is to uproot **(if necessary, emulating the American Revolution and the lessons from its subsequent civil war, by employing the force of moral character and resolve to defeat)** the festering seeds of injustice, official corruption, and petty dictatorship from Nigeria and indeed the whole of Africa.

We refuse to expend energy and time on mere errand boys sent to disrupt our efforts, and distract us from the primary objective. We refuse to be drawn into inefficacious polemics with people who don't even matter.

We have said this before, and we will say it again, Our objective was (and still is) to continue to challenge and embarrass this and any other military dictatorship in Nigeria, and in the process, to motivate, inspire and maybe challenge the moral conscience of all our people (who are not part of this mess) to join forces with us in the pursuit of this common end (for democracy, government accountability, and economic justice in Nigeria).

Our intention was (and still is) not to lash out against our own people in frustration by seeking to beat people into submission until they are seemingly inspired to see the wisdom of our ways, as this and all typical dictatorships are apt to do. If we did, we would not be much better than those we seek to displace.

Having said this, one must caution the Kazaures of this country that from now on, they should be very wary before they call out the dogs again because the next time they do, the fox too may be out prowling, just waiting to pounce.

Make no mistake, we are resolved to have economic justice, political democracy and a better quality of life for All Nigerians, or there may no longer be a Nigeria to be continuously raped and disgraced by these rogues in high places. That is our pledge.

The time for tame protestation is over. If they continue to lash out viciously in desperation we are prepared to match them in resolve. Those who have ears should listen and listen well. The final notice has been served.

TEMPO NEWSPAPPER
18 August, 1994 PUBLISHED OPINION
(REMAINS RELEVANT AND URGENT TODAY)

This Ruling Oligarchy Must Die!

There comes a time in the life of a community when its People must take stock and reflect on the state of the union.

There comes a time indeed when events challenge a people's moral courage; when every man or woman of dignity and conscience is invited to keep an appointed date (of action or apathy) with destiny.

These are times when momentous changes beg for attainment. These are times when old myths no longer mystify. These are times when new legends are made; old foes are vanquished and new friends or foes are respectively canonized or demonized.

These are times when the young come of age, and the rites of passage are complete. New leaders are born. Old heroes with tired bones betray the predictable feet of clay. Seemingly defeated and bitter, they bow to temptation and fall right by the way side. These are difficult times indeed.

Events occur with great rapidity. Myopic leaders of yore are washed away by the massive tide of change, consigned into regional lakes of irrelevance. They flail. They wail. Alas, even they cannot brave the odds and swim to safety out of the murky waters of intrigue they so avidly cultivated.

Today, our country is at a critical cross-read. There really are only two options. We could make progress by going with a course that is right, or we could go seriously wrong by returning to the old ways that continue to cause us so much pain.

We must decide whether we want to continue to abide and be subjected to "Ruler-ship By Appropriation." Now, it matters very little that this appropriation is committed by uninvited and self-serving military busy-bodies, or by cynical self-proclaimed civilian leaders with no discernible constituencies whose resort to electoral fraud is no less heinous.

It is the height of arrogance for a government of military usurpers presuming to have the political legitimacy to charge others (especially those who were properly elected) for Treason. It is even more tragic when you consider that these are just a handful of people who are the puppeteers yanking our chain and pulling our strings to their own insipid delight.

Now let's see, what Imbues Abacha with this kind of blinding courage as he continues in a desperate manner to prop-up his illegitimate regime which is composed of a number of crooks, a few political neophytes, some simpletons and a bunch of "converted progressives"

Obviously, Abacha is relying on brute force to help shore up his position. He forgets however that without the people's goodwill, no amount of fortress of tanks and cheer leading sycophants can immune him or any other usurper when the people decide they've just about had enough.

He should recall the fate that befell his former boss. Heck, he should know, considering that he was once a very trusted Babangida's boy, yet he was very instrumental in ensuring his eventual fall from grace.

In this kind of abasha (mess), there is always a traitor. An Abacha, if you will.

Their hands are soiled and their mouths continue to drip with the oil of corruption. They seek to corrupt the young, and ensnare the weak into this evil cabal so as to effectively silence the voices of protestation, and further delay the arrival of a better orchestrated and very effective opposition to this misrule.

Surely we all know that no messiah is likely to descend in a chariot of fire to help put an end to the practice of despotic madmen clinging to unmerited political power in this country.

No foreign power will lift a finger to gratuitously help to lift our people's burden, if it will not serve its purpose. And as long as we remain intimidated by a few men using a few outdated tanks, some guns and a reluctant army whose families also experience the hardship we all feel, rather than conscript these reluctant soldiers to serve the real mandate of the people, and in effect disarm these thieves so that they are unable to do further harm to this nation and its people.

If our people choose to sit at home and peacefully refuse to submit to their ruler-ship, they will be forced to leave.

If we stand up with pride to fight for a better way of life that we know we deserve, while defiantly accepting the possibility of some casualties, the cause of these greedy usurpers will in a very short time be defeated.

The course we have to embark upon is clear enough. We have to resolve within ourselves if self determination and freedom are important enough goals for us to insist upon.

Like most people, I want to live as long as possible. I want to see my children grow, and pamper their own children as my grandparents did to me.

However, I have made my peace with death. No one lives (in this human flesh) forever. Most of us would like to determine the time, the place and the circumstances of our own demise. We also know that the value of life is not necessarily how long, but how well we lived.

There are things that are worth living for. Indeed, everyone must believe in something; anything, that gives their life meaning and perspective.

That thing has to be unique and valuable that it defines the individual, and should never be lightly forfeited by the individual. For me, as for many other people, it could be expressed in one sentence. The Right To Equal Concern And, Respect as a valuable member of the human race. A guarantee that like others, I will be treated with decency and fairness according to established rules of human conduct.

By insisting on this standard, which is non-negotiable **I am ensuring that my sense of humanity be not diminished. A systemic disregard for this basic natural right challenges the very basis of my humanity, and stabs at my sense of self-worth. If that is taken away from me, I believe l have very little else, and I am diminished indeed.**

Consequently, I am prepared to do whatever is in my power to ensure that this basic right is not lost without a fight. And if I should die while seeking to preserve this right, this essence that defines me, then it was a worthwhile life indeed.

As the saying goes, to each his own. If after reflection, each person determines that his or her condition is unacceptable, the question then is, what is each person so grossly affected willing to do about correcting such an unacceptable anomaly.

For decades, ours have been a legacy of hard life, learning to deal with hard knocks, and sentenced to cope with nothing more than a cycle of hard times.

We are subjected to hard life, hard luck, hard times, and nowhere to go. It makes you wonder what people who refuse to stand up and demand their rights are still afraid of, considering the wretched life and subsistent existence they have already been sentenced to live under. Those who have little to lose really should have very little to fear.

It is those who are benefiting from this unfairness that will be readily opposed to change. Without change, the suffering of our people will continue unabated. It will escalate in time.

We have been over this before. We have gone full circle. I hear even Umaru Dikko, the supercilious Rice Merchant Is back in the saddle again! Now we can really get back to the good old days when our people could actually find something edible to eat from the dust bin of the rich and famous.

Yes, we've had our full cycle of hard times, hard knocks, hard luck, hard life, and it is starting all over again. I refuse to be part of it. You should too. I refuse to be guilty of complicity by inaction.

We should all be prepared to lay it all on the line to stop this nonsense, and if necessary, for the sake of our children and their children's children, be prepared to die trying.

We have passed the age of innocence. The child in us is also dead. The treachery and betrayal of our prior leaders killed it.

The conclusion may seem grave, but I am certain it is obvious to all. They gave us hard times, hard life, hard knocks and a lot of grief. They took lives, our money and our property. Now they seek to completely subdue us into perpetual servitude and slavery. They mean to take away even our most basic right, our dignity. Without question what we have to do is clear. This ruling oligarchy must die. Otherwise, it may be the death of us.

The country remains hostage. How palpable that today, the same oligarchy, barely disguised, remains in charge. And this is well over a decade after the above exhortation and unequivocal challenge to our nation's collective manhood.

Well, the more things seem to be poised for major change in Africa, the more they have painfully stayed the same.

———∿∿°~∘Θ⫸Θ⫷Θ∘~°∘∿∿———

SO, LET'S ATTEMPT ANOTHER TACT BY PROPOSING A MORE INCLUSIVE APPROACH

———∿∿°~∘Θ⫸Θ⫷Θ∘~°∘∿∿———

Let's start off by getting a few things off the table. Let us acknowledge that many in our population, especially the youth who should have been nurtured by a positive social milieu and a constructive and inspiring socio-political and economic system, have been mostly traumatized by the obscene display of unmerited opulence, abject penury and squalor of the population in the midst of plenty and a culture of cynicism and settlement (Nigeria's version of 'KALABULE'?).

So to the legitimately abused and put upon, yes, you are Victims of infamy. May your spirit be consoled. May your heart be healed. May your pain be assuaged.

For some of you who have lost loved ones as a direct (or indirect) result of Africa's corrupt political system, I am truly empathetic about your loss.

At a certain level, I probably cannot begin to understand
Your sense of loss
And deep sorrow

However, I hope
That you will somehow
Find solace
In knowing that
There are people
Who genuinely empathize
And care

WE ARE ALL ULTIMATELY IN THE SAME BOAT AND ON THIS PROFOUND HUMAN JOURNEY TOGETHER.

SO

As difficult and hopeless
As it may seem right now
Time has a divine way
Of helping us deal better
With difficult and painful circumstances
Stay strong.

FINALLY,
TO THOSE STILL STRADDLING THE FENCE OF INDECISION
Whenever you're ready
TO JOIN THE BATTLE
WHENEVER YOU'RE READY TO FIGHT BACK
AND JETTISSON VICTIMHOOD
Many of us who care about you
Will still be here waiting
To support you
Any way you want

TO THOSE WHO LOST LOVED ONES TO RECENT POLITICAL
UPRISINGS

May God heal your wounded heart
And apply his balm to soothe
Your disconsolate spirit
And hopefully timely re-energize you
From your understandable
But dangerously expensive stupor!

SUFFER THE 'NOT SO LITTLE' CHILDREN

We must keep our faith in the coming generation; even young adults who currently are too greedy, naive or fatally distracted to recognize who their true friends and heroes are.

The cross of the adult is to sometimes suffer the ignorance and wasted energy of the youth, even as they snuggle closer to persons or circumstances that are blatantly inimical to their interests!

Yes
These strapping lads of ours
Innocent and untested
Vigorous and dogged as they attempt to relish
The flavorless swig from the eternal fountain vine
That each must swallow down pipes untested
And imbibe with panache for effect as they embellish

TO THE YOUTH WHO STILL BELIEVE

If you believe it
And you work hard at it
You'll probably achieve it
This is wishing you all the best
As you strive with courage to better your best

A CHALLENGE TO THE YOUTHS OF AFRICA

Live with passion
Don't let anyone fashion
A design
That causes you to resign
From dreaming big dreams
Or striving to live out your dreams

CIRCA 2001-

ON BEHALF OF THE RAMPAGING YOUTHS IN ONE OF THE STATES IN THE OLD WESTERN REGION, IN AN EFFORT TO BRING PEACE, AND HOPEFULLY, A MEASURE OF POLITICAL SENSITIVITY AND MEETING OF THE MINDS BETWEEN THE PEOPLE AND THEIR ELECTED LEADERS, I WROTE AND ALSO MET WITH SEVERAL PEOPLE, INCLUDING THOSE AT THE HIGHEST LEVELS OF GOVERNMENT IN THE STATE.

I PERSONALLY EXHORTED THEM TO CONSTRUCTIVELY TAP INTO THE ENERGY OF THE YOUTH AND BRING THEM AND THEIR ISSUES TO THE FOREFRONT OF A PEOPLE-ORIENTED SET OF PROGRAMS THEREBY MEETING THEIR LEGITIMATE NEEDS WHILE ALSO USING THAT TO BUILD A POSITIVE POLITICAL LEGACY FOR THEMSELVES.

BETWEEN 1999 AND 2007, OTHER DIRECT AND INDIRECT INITIATIVES AND IDEAS WERE COMMUNICATED BY ME AND OTHERS TO OTHER POLITICAL FIGURES AROUND THE COUNTRY (WITHOUT REGARD TO POLITICAL PARTY). THESE WERE PEOPLE WHO COULD HAVE MADE A DIFFERENCE IN THE PEOPLE'S LIVES.

I WILL LEAVE IT TO HISTORY AND INDEPENDENT OBSERVERS TO DETERMINE WHETHER THESE STATESMANLIKE INITIATIVES WERE HEEDED.

INDEED, IT WAS PARTLY THE INSENSITIVITY OF THE PROFESSIONAL POLITICIANS TO THE PEOPLE'S PLIGHT, THEIR ARROGANCE AND OBTUSENESS WHICH EVENTUALY CAUSED ME (AND A FEW OTHERS) TO RELUCTANTLY DECIDE TO ENGAGE MYSELF MORE DIRECTLY IN PARTISAN POLITICS BY STANDING FOR OFFICE AND POINTEDLY PITTING MY TENT WITH A RELATIVELY NEWER POLITICAL OUTFIT THAT HAD NOT YET TARNISHED ITS REPUTATION IN THE STATE!

To my legion of supporters and other progressive friends, GIVEN THE 2007 ELECTORAL DEBACLE, we obviously have much work left to do.

I just want you to know
That I believe in you
And that I remain committed
We each must therefore resolve
To do anything
To ultimately make positive change happen
I hope you feel the same way

This is wishing you Godspeed
And courage
As you do your part
In pursuit of these salutary dreams
May all our dreams come true
I wish you all the inspiration
To be the best
You can be

FORGIVENESS FOR THE CORRUPTED YOUTH

In this bitter and cold season of discontent

Of anger and disappointment

Borne out of mistakes or misunderstandings

I readily forgive those who are now sincerely repentant and are prepared to change their wayward ways going forward in this dialectic battle for the soul of Africa.

LIFE

It's not about the accumulated possessions you cannot take with you. It's about the more ENDURING Legacy! OR IS IT?

So
What is life about?
We trudge in a round about
Manner to attain straight forward goals
We hope are replete with gold
Mined in the fog of our clouded minds' eye
And we vie
Again and again we vie

To take a swig of this lively drink
Before we sink
To be born again, we think
In the eternal chain that links
But is this rite of passage that is seemingly without end
Designed to fulfill meaningful end
Or are we perchance
Mere sorry puppets in a blindly contrived game of chance
That only bears meaning
To our active imagination hungry for some meaning
Of all the fuss and ambitious exertions
And the grasp at this formless essence and life's exertions
And as we came upon its impenetrable cage of steel
That essence and meaning appear elusive still
We think
Or perhaps the secret of the link
Is there before us to behold
And finally be told
Even as it recedes to the very brink
Of the many moments we collectively choose to blink
Think!

I believe it's time for the next generation of YOUNG LEADERS to prove their mettle!

Through the tentative impressions
Left by the waddling
Little motions
Of tiny infants
Who with time
Thankfully grow
Into adulthood
Are soon discovered
The indelibly bold prints
Of giants
Even on the very core
Of the eternally shifting
Sands of time

It will not be easy. The road will be rocky. However, I have no doubt that we can effect CHANGE if we really want! We must therefore persevere in our collective DEFIANCE!

Yes
They may shield US from the sun
And the view of those
Who would with kindness and love
Cast their gaze upon US
Still, WE survive
Even as they rebuke the wind
That races forth to soothe US
And nestle beneath OUR wings
As WE seek to soar toward OUR exalted destiny
Away from where they hope WE stay defeated
To cool OUR heels
Still, WE survive
Alas, they may deprive US of water
That life preserving sustenance
That moistens OUR lips and OUR very sinew
Even as they cast US out to sea
'Water boarded' with the Ocean's undrinkable water
Still, WE survive
Yes, WE survive
Like the cat with nine times nine lives
WE survive and defy them, even as WE revel in life's fortunes
The sun shines brightly to glorify OUR wake
On golden wings WE survive
And remain
Defiant, still

A REQUIEM FOR A DEFUNCT COLONIAL MENTALITY
(As We Redirect the Brain Drain)

So, if you must,
Let's go to London
Before we're done
And let's come alive again
With a game

Let's go to Paris
With a flourish
Let's stay in France
And paint it red with Francs

Let's go to Rome
And let our imagination roam
Let's cater to our soul, once famished and cold
Let's reach out to destiny's gold

Yes, let's go to London
Before we're done
Let's take our shiny Francs
To France
And finally to Rome
We'll go and find a roomy home
To roam

SO, LET'S GET THIS ITCH OUT OF OUR SYSTEM SO WE CAN ACT WITH PURPOSE, WITH FOCUS AND RESOLVE!

Why not us? Our people deserve the good life too. Don't they?

So, for goodness sake

Reach for the sky
Touch the yellow moon high
Float with the birds
Angel wings aboard

Reach for the sky
Let your soul fly
High into the heavens o'er
The deep blue clouds soar

Reach for the sky
Rise and reach far high
Feel the breeze and fly
With the Angels, the birds fly

The following represent my proposed cautionary instructions (or anthems) for the young and the potentially 'wobbly', lest they completely lose their way

WHEN

When you are able to remain forthright
Even though it impairs your desires
When you can stare at your face in the mirror
And confidently admit you did your best

When your word is truly your bond
Uncompromised merely to win the moment
And others behind your back can swear
In reliance on the assurances you have made

When you can stand tall and admit
That the things you once held immutable are wrong
And still walk away unbowed
But refreshed and refocused by your new admission

When you can identify the things to change
And be wily about how and when to effect the change
And still take pride in the remaining merits of your cause
Without being defensive, despondent or disparaging

When you can truly free yourself
From the trap and trappings of reputation and office
When you can really learn to listen to other's point of view
And freely admit a virtue in your ardent adversary

When you finally learn to be wary
Of the discreet demons in your sanctuary
Then and only then may you lay claim to the blessings of wisdom
That have transcended through the ages

PEACE

Healthy aspiration tempered by contentment
Admiration without avarice
Love of the company of others
Without completely losing your mind or identity

Precluding money to be your master
Or its acquisition your singular aim
To appreciate a good joke
Especially the ones made at your expense

To strive to have a good life
To be honest with yourself
To resist the temptation of allowing success to rule you
And never take yourself too seriously

Avoid people who are too enamored
With the sound of their own voice

Endeavor to be a good listener
And share your wisdom with the world

Don't go out of your way to do harm
If possible, settle differences immediately
While you may use others for inspiration
Never define your worth through their eyes

Love yourself and the things you care about
Dwell little on the prospect of death
So far as we know, it is inevitable
Don't take it as a personal affront

Now for a brief reality check. Recall how some ambitious folks who thought they could use the funds and political connections of dubious political godfathers without dancing to the dictated political tune learned their lessons the hard way.

From Ngige—Uba and Obasanjo axis; the Adedibu, Ladoja, Akala and the other acolytes in Oyo State to AD, AC, ACD, AFENIFERE and the unraveling Adamawa Mafia coalition. You could almost pick a State, any State. And you could see the unraveling of a godfather-godson relationship after the prize has been won and the godson begins to chafe under the suddenly **'unreasonable'** demands of the godfather, as if the implicit and often corrupt expectation of a blatant quid pro quo was a total surprise!

Decades ago, **it used to matter HOW someone came about a sudden wealth.** Now, no one seems to care. In fact, most folks fully expect to steal, trick, scheme or illicitly contrive their way into a quick ill-gotten wealth (like the new 'national heroes', the profligate politicians who are actually being celebrated for muscling and stealing and lying their way to the spoils!)

One of the effective ways of curbing the 'godfather syndrome' is by NOT rewarding those who rig their way to office; By imposing a set of strict election and campaign finance rules with some real teeth; And by

ensuring a timely disposition of adjudicated election matters, rather than the deliberately slow pace adopted by some judges (probably waiting to instigate an auction for their ultimate verdicts).

Justice delayed is justice denied!

When corrupt politicians know that the worse that would happen when they rig is for the VERY SLOW WHEELS OF JUSTICE EITHER TO BE TOO SKITTISH AND AFRAID TO SUMMARILY REMOVE THEM FROM UNMERITED ASCENSCION, OR WHEN IT DARES TO DO SO IN SELECTED CASES, TO DO SO ONE TO TWO YEARS AFTER THEY'VE BEEN SWORN INTO OFFICE AND ENJOYED THE PERQUISITES OF OFFICE THEY SHOULD NEVER HAVE BEEN ALLOWED TO TASTE!

The court system must promptly help to redress this by putting an appeal process in place that allows for substantial justice and to render the FINAL verdicts timely AND BEFORE ANYONE IS SWORN IN (except in very narrowly defined exceptional circumstances).

"Whatever strains with force will ultimately break and decay . . . In all of nature, no storm can last forever. Therefore, if heaven and earth cannot sustain a forced action, how much less is a man or group of men able to do? Those who follow the way of wisdom become one with the way. Those who elect to stray ultimately become one with failure. We do not need rules, protocols or ceremony to act virtuously toward others. When society falls into chaos, official loyalists appear and the verbal celebration of 'patriotism' is soon unleashed."—Wisdom of the TAO

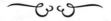

3.

NAMING NAMES

(A) FIRST, SOME GOOD NEWS!

The number one duty of any civilized government is to provide both external and internal security for its citizens.

So it gladdens one's heart when one finds incidences of constructive collaboration between governmental entities, especially when such collaborating entities are headed by persons belonging to rival political parties. It is even more remarkable when one of them is still smarting from recent violence and retribution from the last national elections.

It also shows the potential for public-private partnerships that would be needed in order to significantly improve the socio-economic fortunes of the average citizen in the country.

According to the published report in the DAILY INDEPENDENT of August 5, 2008 filed by Kingsley Ighomenghian and Funmi Falobi who were reporting from Lagos Nigeria, President Yar'Adua approved joint military patrol for Lagos in an effort to improve the state of security in the commercial capital of the country.

The newspaper reported that; "Lagosians have had their security boosted by a total donation of N1.66 billion from banks and other corporate bodies; it emerged on Monday, as **President Umaru Yar'Adua** approved in Abuja a Joint Military Patrol (JMP) of the land, sea and waterways in the state.

Governor Babatunde Fashola broke the news of the Presidential approval at the second town hall meeting on security and the re-launch of the state's Security Trust Fund in Lagos.

He said the JMP will enable the state to equip the Navy, Army and the police with logistics and materials.

He also spoke of plans to install Closed Circuit Television (CCTV) cameras all over the state to detect and monitor crime.

It would take-off after the completion of the security command centre that would process the information gathered by the cameras, he added.

Fashola appealed to corporate organizations which have enjoyed improved security in the last 12 months to buy into the initiative and donate to the Fund.

He disclosed that beyond the purchase of communication gadgets and arms and ammunition, the money received from corporate donors last year was used Armoured Personnel Carriers (APCS) vehicles, back-up fleet ballistic gears and equipment for the Rapid Response Squad (RRS).

He said the security reforms would not be limited to the payment of an additional salary of N25, 000 to any policeman posted to the state, but would also ensure the rebuilding of police formations".

"We intend to build a model Area Command for Area C and gradually upscale to other Area Commands in the state from where we can also go to the Divisional Offices," he explained.

Police Commissioner, Marcel Akpovibo, noted that crime rate has reduced drastically since the state government took the initiative to retool the police, stressing that he has read the riot act to his officers that the mission statement henceforth is zero tolerance to crime and other vices. Akpoyibo said with the equipment as well as support from the government, his men have forced criminals to the fringes such as Ikorodu, Epe and Badagry, which shows that they are on their way out of the state.

But he sought additional materials and equipment that would enable the police do more.

The Chairman of the Board of Trustees of the Fund, Femi Makanjuola, noted that the public-private sector partnership used by the government in tackling the neglect of the police has impacted positively as Lagos has recorded remarkable improvements in policing since the Fund was created last year.

The Executive Secretary of the Fund, Fola Arthur-Worrey, reiterated that although money has been used to provide equipment, the Fund is being tasked by other requests made by the police.

He listed, among others, the demand for two 350 KVA generators by the Police Hospital in Falomo, the payment of rent arrears and financing of the purchase of a property for the Bode Thomas police station.

The state government disclosed that the Security Fund has received a total of N1.661 billion in form of donations from the state and its agencies, banks and other corporate bodies.

The trustees also reported an expenditure of N1.10 billion in their six months' score-card, according to Governor **Fashola**.

Arthur-Worrey told the stakeholders in his report that there is need to solicit more support as the Fund is left with about N165 million and a plethora of demands.

A breakdown of the donations shows that members of the Lagos State Executive Council and the state's federal lawmakers contributed N22 million while private organisations and individuals pooled N811.019 million. **Zenith Bank, Access Bank, Union Bank, Intercontinental Bank, United Bank for Africa, First Bank, Stanbic IBTC Bank and Nigeria International Bank donated about N515.419 million.**

Vehicles and security equipment worth N828.107 million came from the state government, **First Bank, Zenith Bank, Oceanic Bank International, Intercontinental Bank, Diamond Bank and Guaranty Trust Bank. Others include Fidelity Bank, Skye Bank, Sterling Bank, Ecobank Nigeria, Standard Chartered Bank, Churchgate Group and Elizade Nigeria.**

Arthur-Worrey's report noted that the bulk of the amount has been spent on projects like the RRS, contact centre management solution services, supply and installation of security gadgets, patrol vans, and installation of communication sets, among others.

TO BE SURE THERE ARE A FEW FEEL GOOD STORIES IN OUR POLITICAL LIFE IN RECENT YEARS THAT SHOULD BE CELEBRATED.

FOR EXAMPLE, THE IMPRESSIVE SPINE BEING SHOWN BY A NUMBER OF JUDGES, INCLUDING THOSE WHO HAD THE COURAGE TO INVALIDATE A NUMBER OF THE FRAUDULENT ELECTION RESULTS ANNOUNCED BY INEC, THEREBY FACING DOWN (IN MOST CASES) THE AFFECTED RULING PARTY EITHER AT THE NATIONAL OR STATE LEVEL, NOT WITHSTANDING THE PARTY'S ABILITY TO INTIMIDATE OR BRIBE LAVISHLY WITH THE NATION'S 'ALLOCATED' RESOURCES.

So far, **Governor Fashola of Lagos State** is also proving to be a comparatively more sophisticated and focused helmsman. The ongoing initiative to clean up and ultimately beautify certain areas of the State shows a forward looking and holistic approach to governance.

The hope is that the initiative will be extended statewide (beyond the predictable 'high brow' areas of the state) in order to have the desired effect long term. It is the only way to reverse decades of neglect that effectively turned much of this once great state into an overcrowded series of ghettos and shanty towns. If done right, the potential health savings and attendant socio-economic benefits inherent in the ongoing initiatives can therefore not be overstated.

SYSTEMIC CORRUPTION AS PART OF THE NATIONAL ETHOS

Lanre Adewole reported in The NIGERIAN TRIBUNE edition of August 5, 2008 on how government officials collected twenty two million naira (N22m) bribe from job applicants during Immigration and the Prisons department recruitment efforts. Five (5) officials were subsequently arrested by the ICPC, one of the major crime fighting entities in the country.

According to the report;

"As investigation continues into the death of 43 applicants during recruitment tests conducted by two main agencies in the Ministry of Interior, the Independent Corrupt Practices and Other Related Offences Commission on Monday in Abuja revealed how a syndicate in the ministry collected over N22 million bribes from 140 applicants".

A statement from the commission and signed by its Spokes-person, Mr. Sina Babasola, disclosed that five members of the syndicate had been arrested and undergoing interrogation.

The statement read: "A special syndicate which specialises in demanding and collecting money from prospective applicants seeking employment into the Nigeria Prisons Service (NPS) and Nigeria Immigrations Service (NIS) has been smashed by operatives of the Independent Corrupt Practices and Other Related Offences Commission (ICPC). "The leader of the syndicate, a Chief Superintendent of Prison, Mrs. Mba Josephine Uchenna, attached to the Administration Department of the NPS, has been arrested by the commission in connection with the alleged scam."

(1)

ADVANCE FEE FAUD:—NIGERIA AS THE 419 CAPITAL OF THE WORLD—STILL?

THE FOLLOWING IS A COPY OF A FEW OF THE DOZENS OF PAGES OF 419 SOLICITATIONS FAXED TO MY PRIVATE OFFICE IN THE UNITED STATES ALL BETWEEN JULY AND OCTOBER OF 2008.

WITH THE EFCC AND THE ICPC CRIME FIGHTING UNITS— AREN'T WE SUPPOSED TO HAVE TURNED THIS CORNER?

Incidentally, this is about the tenth or so letter of this type I have received over the past seventeen years.

I also recall that around 1991, I saved clients of the law firm I worked for in the USA potential losses that could have ranged in the millions.

After I dispatched my own investigative team to travel round Nigeria to get to the bottom of what I considered then to be a suspicious trap emanating from the offices of some of the highest officials in government who, being privy to a multi-million dollar deal tried to set up the foreign contractors whose interests the firm was representing.

Despite the apparent collusion of some government officials and police officers at the time, I was able to determine that it was a fraud and the firm promptly advised the client accordingly.

Well, as many of our international friends are finding out, '419' (AS THE ADVANCE FEE FRAUD SCHEME IS FONDLY NICKNAMED IN NIGERIA) is largely dependent on the GREED, CARELESSNESS or GULLIBILITY of the potential victim.

Please read closely in case you get a similar letter. **And by the way, I encourage law enforcement folks (AROUND THE WORLD) to note the listed phone (and fax) number(s) in case they could employ it to track down this particular syndicate.**

Will someone pleas catch them and put them away for very long prison terms before they do further harm to others and the much sullied reputation of Nigeria and its mostly decent people?

JUST TAKE A LOOK AT THE ENCLOSED SAMPLING OF THE MANY RIDICULOUS MATERIALS FORWARDED (BY FAX TO ME) IN ORDER TO ENTICE AND WICKEDLY ENTRAP ME.

THE CROOKS THAT RUN THESE BILLION DOLLAR ENTERPRISE COUNT ON HUMAN GULLIBILITY, GREED OR A CERTAIN LACK OF SOPHISTICATION OR NEGLIGENCE WITH ONE'S OWN PERSONAL INFORMATION.

HOPEFULLY THE ENCLOSED INFORMATION WILL ALERT OTHERS TO THE KINDS OF BAIT BEING EMPLOYED BY THESE SO-CALLED 'YAHOO-BOYS' THAT HAVE GIVEN NIGERIA A VERY BADREPUTATION AROUNDTHE WORLD!

THE PRESIDENCY
DEBT RECONCILIATION COMMITTEE
TEL 2 34-808-9427906   FAX 23 4-1-5559348

ATTN: Contract Beneficiary.

IMMEDIATE CONTRACT PAYMENT.CONTRACT #: GVRCBN/NNPC/FGN/MIN/008

I am directed by PRESIDENT UMARU MUSA YARADUA President of the Federal Republic of Nigeria to bring to your immediate notice and urgent attention that this new Government understands your plight, the huge amount of money you have spent and all th disappointment you have suffered in the past to get your contract fund paid to you.

I wish to inform you that your payment is being processed and will be released to you as soon as you respond to this letter. Also note that from the record in my file your outstandin contract payment is is $15.5 million dollars (fifteen million five hundred thousand united states dollars). With due respect sir, do re-confirm to me if this is not inline with what you have in your record and also re-confirm to me the followings

1) your full name.(2) Phone, fax and mobile number.
3) Company name, position and address. (4) Profession, age and marital status.
5) Copy of your int'l passport.

As soon as this information is received, your payment will be made in a certified bank draf cash payment or k.t.t wired to your bank account directly from Central Bank of Nigeria an a copy of payment slips / draft will be given to you for you to take to your bank and confirmation depending on your choice payment.

This morning a Telex Signal attached with a Presidential Instruction Stamped and Signed The President have being sent to (CBN) to contact you for the payment of your Contract Fund and two other Contractors within 48 Hours. You are however, strongly advised for tl interest of your person, your esteemed Company to Contact me, Chairman, Contract Awai Committee, DR PAUL SULE. on Tel: 234-808-9427906. Fax: 234-1-5559348 or Email: paul_sule1000@yahoo.com, for the Immediate payment of your Contract Fund within the next 48 Banking Hours

Regard

DR PAUL SULE
DEBT RECONCILIATION COMMITTEE
Telephone: 234-808-9427906

OFFICE OF THE PRESIDENCY
Aso - Rock Villa Abuja

Ref: ASO-ROCK/PGN/CP/2709/08

Sir,   <u>STOP ALL COMMUNICATIONS</u>

08th October, 2008.

I am **MR. MICHEAL DUKE**, Chairman Debt Reconciliation Committee of the office of the presidency, I have been directed by His Excellency, the President of the Federal Republic of Nigeria **(ALHAJI UMARU MUSA YAH'ADUA), SFF, GCRF)**, to bring to your immediate notice and urgent attention that this new Government understand your plight, the huge amount of money you have spent and all the disappointments you have suffered in the past to get your contract fund paid to you. Due to what we described as selective payment and incessant demand of excessive fee by some unscrupulous and corrupt erstwhile officials in charge of foreign contract payment in the past.

However, upon assumption of office by this Democratic Elected Government, series of special meeting were held home and abroad with some leaders of the World Monetary Institution e.g. World Bank Group, International Monetary Fund **(IMF)** Paris and London Club of Creditors, European Economic Community (**E .E. C.**) And envoy's of our Correspondence International Bank of Settlement Worldwide affiliated with the Central Bank of Nigeria. The purpose of this special meeting is to (I) rebuild Nigeria Economy (II) pay all Foreign Debts. In this regards, and due to the good and positive results we receive from this special meeting a Total sum of **US$2.3 Billion U.S. Dollars** have been approved from the supplementary Budget Bill which was approved by the Upper House of assembly recently to pay all foreign Contractors whose payment have been hanging since 1989.

Be informed that your name has be listed among 10 (TEN) fund Beneficiaries whose payment instruction has been raised. This morning a Telex Signal attached with a Presidential Instruction Stamped and Signed by the President have being sent to the CONTRACT PAYMENT PANEL (**CPP**) for the payment of your Contract Fund and nine other Contractors within 48 hours. Be informed that all contractors concern must obtain a copy of his/her certificate of indemnity.

You are advised as a matter of urgency to contact the CONTRACT PAYMENT PANEL headed by Mr. Effiong Bassey on telephone numbers: 234-1-7657334, Mobile: 234-808-9598383 Or E-mail: cppnlg@yahoo.com with the following information's:

    (a)   Your Company name and address
    (b)   Your Telephone and fax numbers
    (c)   Your Contract number and amount
    (d)   Your Receiving bank information.

Sir, on behalf of this Democratic Government of Nigeria, I apologize for any delay you might have encountered in receiving your fund in the past. However, **Congratulations in advance!**

Yours faithfully,

MR. MICHEAL DUKE
CHAIRMAN DEBT RECONCILIATION COMMITTEE
FEDERAL GOVERNMENT OF NIGERIA

(2)

CORRUPTION IN HIGH PLACES

Of course when the head is rotten, the whole body is liable to be equally so. How the 1999, 2003 and the 2007 elections were successively rigged (and yet tolerated and accorded legitimacy by the international community) should have alerted the nation that things have not changed much for the better, despite decades of military rule. Our politicians (and their local and international sponsors), still very much corrupt remain undeterred in subverting our people's will.

Indications at the inception of the then new civilian government gave close observers great pause. It started with persons elected to high office (even the PDP anointed Speaker of the federal house of Representatives) being discovered to have presented FORGED DOCUMENTS in order to qualify to contest the elections. After the fall of that young Speaker, many others with similar issues promptly paid off those they need to pay off in order to help them validate dubious documents. And so the battle was joined for the race to the bottom.

Even **the great Chief Gani Fawehinmi** was heckled and shouted down by people who should know better, claiming we should overlook some inconvenient evidence of fraud and lack of a required qualification by some of the favored candidates in order **"to give the nascent democracy a chance."**

Well, I guess we are now where we are because we laid the foundation of the new democracy on a fatally flawed (muddy) foundation as the GREAT ZIK OF AFRICA fervently warned us against during his day.

Shortly thereafter, a number of elected officials at both the national and state levels were found to be involved in shady contract deals, including out right conversion of federal and state funds.

Yet, somehow, the system was pliable enough for them to finesse the issues, avoid accountability and still retain their positions.

THE PROGNOSIS WAS DIRE. THE NEW DEMOCRACY SOON BECAME A SEAMY CESSPOOL OF INTRIGUE AND CORRUPTION.

IT PROMPTLY BECAME UNWORTHY OF ANY PERSON WITH
INTEGRITY AND POSITIVE VISION.

**WELL, PERHAPS THAT WAS THE POINT. TO EFFECTIVELY
DISMAY AND KEEP THE POLITICAL "SAINTS" AFFLICTED
WITH THE 'AWOLOWO SYNDROME' OUT.**

**THEY PARTICULARLY DEPLORED THOSE WHO TIRESOMELY
INSISTED ON PROJECTING AND ADVOCATING FOR PUBLIC
PROBITY AND PROGRAMATIC COHERENCE BY ASPIRING
OFFICE SEEKERS.**

**BUT WHAT ELSE SHOULD WE EXPECTED WHEN THE 1999
CONCOCTED CONSTITUTION WAS NOT EVEN OFFICIALLY
ISSUED (BY MILITARY FIAT) UNTIL AFTER THE ELECTIONS!!!**

Well, as part of my research for this Book, I came across a compelling (and
in retrospect, a rather ironic and sadly prophetic) piece entitled **HOW TO
BUY A SENATOR** written by **Sonala Olumhense** and published in the
November 24, 2002 edition of THE GUARDIAN.

In it, he referenced the bribery incident involving some three hundred
(#300,000,000) million Naira allegedly offered by the Obasanjo
Administration through Senator Arthur Nzeribe to members of the nation's
Senate to squelch (the then) President Obasanjo's pending impeachment
for some unconstitutional actions.

Quoting Olumhense;

"If anyone were tempted to forget the Crown Prince of Political Controversy,
Chief Nzeribe has reintroduced himself to our nation.

If you understand his story correctly, the impeachment threat against
President Olusegun Obasanjo has been bought, and paid for.

In the version told by the maverick (senator), the price was 300 million
Naira, and of that figure, 60 million went to the Senate President and his
supporters, while other Senators picked up three million apiece. The Senators

accuse the Imo State Senator, himself the subject of an earlier corruption "investigation" in the House, of lying.

. . . On the table is an attempt to impeach the President of the Federal Republic. He faces assorted charges of constitutional violations, to which he has responded, part in jest, part in imperious earnestness. Lately, there has been no official word on the matter, and an impeachment threat that was beginning to boil over had magically begun to disappear.

In such circumstances, Nzeribe's 300 million Naira refreshments in the upper chamber begins to put things into a different perspective, and it would be difficult to persuade the Nigerian voter that nothing untoward has taken place . . . **Let us look on the bright side. One reason that we have been unable to make progress in this country is that corruption at the highest levels has never been punished.**

The nation's wallet is spent buying favours rather than answering the popular will, and no one is ever brought to book.

The impeachment of a President would be a shock to our young democracy, but it would be a welcome shock, the kind that is good for the system if the objective is to ensure that the constitution is honoured in the future. Corruption in the Senate at this level, should it be proved, would be devastating.

Who would you trust to make law for you if supposedly respectable Nigerians can be bought for the price of a used car? In the future, how much would be required to persuade them to (give) away entire local councils or institutions?

As the drama unfolds, there is a move in the Senate to fold up the anti-graft commission, which has begun to investigate aspects of the cesspit.

In the House of Representatives, Speaker Ghali Umar Na'abba has also taken the Commission, which is headed by Justice Mustapha Akanbi, to court over its investigations of the petition of Chief Nzeribe.

Two issues stand out here. First of all, it is comforting that our legislators find that when trouble beckons, they do trust the judiciary to render

justice. This is ironic, since we elect our legislators in the understanding that we can count on their integrity. Now, what if the judge also wants to buy a used car?

The second issue is more important than pocketing freshly printed Naira bills. Since 1999, a pattern of institutionalized looting has emerged in the federal legislature, a pattern where legislators have redefined the business of lawmaking in terms of how many private contracts can be distributed. **Even in-house reports emanating from the place have made this shameful point and implicated many members, but nobody has been decent enough yet even to resign.**

It is important to recognize that the Nzeribe fork on the highway is only one milestone. It is not the journey. Eventually, enough of the shenanigans will be uncovered to set the picture straight.

For every legislator that wants to cheat Nigerians, the first thing would be to find a leaf big enough under which to hide, and hope that that leaf neither rots nor is blown away. It is also perfectly in order to try to buy journalists or judges or silence; all you have to do is making certain there is enough room under that leaf to hold you and your secrets. If you do not, that leaf will be removed, and it will be replaced with a grave either for you or for your political reputation."

Well, as Sonala and patriots like him would have noticed, between 1999 and now, our corrupt politicians have grown more sure-footed and emboldened in their shenanigans.

Also, with all that unregulated cash flow and absolute lack of accountability, the tempting orgy has ensnared many of our very amenable judges and law enforcement officials. And with the wisdom gleaned from the past, including the fiasco of the 1983 #2.8 Billion Naira 'investigation' of Obasanjo's regime (or the Gulf WAR Oil Windfall during Babangida's regime) when too many facts were allowed to leak to the public, our corrupt politicians now have a better grip on how to make 'developing information disappear or how to render pertinent facts fuzzier by the day, just enough to render them debatable at best. And lord knows we love our parlor debates in Nigeria!

Let me close this section with a quote from the Sunday Comment published in the November 11, 2002 of THIS DAY Newspaper **(who, strangely between late 2006 and early 2007, suffered some major tragedies I hope have been diligently looked into, including the death of its editor and having its offices completely gutted by fire around the time it was having a stand off with the government on some national issues!)**

Senate of Shame!

"It was one shame too many for the nation's upper legislative chamber last Thursday when the bribery allegations currently rocking it took a new dimension. Controversial Senator Arthur Nzeribe made a fresh allegation, accusing Senate President Anyim Pius Anyim of collecting N60 million bribe from him to abort the impeachment moves against President Olusegun Obasanjo. Nzeribe himself had earlier been suspended indefinitely for allegedly defrauding the Senate to the tune of N22 million and forgery.

Addressing a press conference on Thursday with the aim of clearing allegations of forgery made against him, Nzeribe denied stealing the Senate's money. Rather, he claimed it was the whole Senate that should probe itself as most of his colleagues were enmeshed in corruption.

Apart from accusing Anyim, he also said the deputy Senate President, Alhaji Ibrahim Mantu, assisted him in distributing N300 million so that they could scuttle the impeachment moves. He further alleged that Senators queued, signed and collected the N3 million bribes, but were not privy to the source of the money.

A few weeks before this episode, Senator Mamman Ali had made a similar allegation, accusing some of his colleagues of collecting N3 million naira each to back off from Obasanjo's impeachment.

Nzeribe now claims that he is corroborating Mamman's allegation and that it was because of Anyim's involvement in the bribery and corruption saga that the Senate refused to take any action when Mamman brought the matter up.

However, in a swift reaction, Mantu denied ever helping Nzeribe in the distribution of money to Senators for the purpose of making them go against Obasanjo's impeachment.

Similarly, Senate spokesman, Dr. Jonathan Zwingina, described Nzeribe's allegation as an "absolute falsehood coming from the mouth of a drowning person" and challenged him to name the source of the bribe money and where he gave it to those he allegedly reached.

Whatever may be the truth of the allegations and counter-allegations, what should be noted is that Nigerians are really perplexed by the frequency of corruption scandal coming from their supposedly most dignified and respectable legislative chamber.

This is the same Senate which in the last three and half-years of its existence has had to change leadership three times over corruption scandals. For the Senate to again get enmeshed in another corruption allegation is not only nauseating, it is indeed demeaning and dishonourable.

The Senate in a presidential democracy is supposed to be a repository of honour, integrity, distinction and wisdom. Not many Nigerians will vouch that our Senate has lived up to these expectations.

We recall the certificate scandal that first rocked the leadership at its inception and later the allegations of financial misappropriation and embezzlement which led to the impeachment of the second Senate President as well as indictment of several Senators.

Recently, the same Senate got itself caught in an ignoble act when it pardoned members who had been found guilty of corruption by the Idris Kuta's panel. Such has been the build-up that has now earned the upper chamber so much disrespect and dishonour from the public.

The Senate has, however, not been alone in this mess. The House of Representatives is similarly notorious. But if the Senate can not earn its integrity, how can the House of Representatives get a model to follow or where to derive its moral strength?

It is our view that both the allegations against Nzeribe for forgery and embezzlement as well as his counter-allegation of bribery and corruption against Anyim and other members be thoroughly investigated. The Senate must direct the Inspector General of Police to prosecute Nzeribe if it is really sure of its fact. Similarly, Nzeribe must be invited by the security agencies to prove his very serious allegations.

The issue of corruption is one major obstacle to the nation's socio-economic development. It discourages foreign investment, gives the nation and its citizenry a very bad image in the eyes of the civilized world and stifles economic growth.

The (current) democracy was to hasten the process of a renewal and our law makers are supposed to be in the forefront of that effort. But rather than do this, they themselves have turned the perpetrators of corruption, preferring only to fight the cankerworm when their personal interests have been injured. Enough is enough"!

INCIDENTALLY, NONE OF THESE ACTORS EVER FACED A CRIMINAL PROSECUTION, MUCH LESS GO TO JAIL FOR THIS AND OTHER SUBSEQUENT INCIDENTS THAT WERE CONSISTENTLY SWEPT UNDER THE CARPET.

FURTHER, ON THE RARE OCASSION THAT TOO MUCH FACTS HAD LEAKED OUT REGARDING A FEW OF THE WELL PLACED POLITICIANS, INCLUDING A COUPLE OF FORMER SENATE PRESIDENTS, ARRANGEMENTS WERE MADE TO ENSURE THEY WERE GIVEN (in Nigerian parlance), "A SOFT LANDING"!

YEP. THE COUNTRY STILL HAS DIFFERENT RULES OF ACCOUNTABILTY FOR THE AVERAGE CITIZENS AND ANOTHER SET OF RULES FOR THE REST OF NIGERIAN SOCIETY THAT CONSIDERS ITSELF ABOVE THE LAW, THEREBY MAKING NIGERIA A COUNTRY NOT RULED BY LAWS BUT BY THE WHIMS OF MEN IN HIGH PLACES.

SO, UNTIL THIS FUNDAMENTAL ANOMALY IS CORRECTED THROUGH OUR TIRELESS AND COLLECTIVE EFFORTS, WE DELUDE OURSELVES IF WE BELIEVE THAT OTHER COSMETIC EXERTIONS WILL RESULT IN THE KINDS OF CHANGES WE SEEK!

(3)

(a) CORRUPTION IN LOW PLACES—THE DAY I WEPT FOR NIGERIA

SYSTEMIC CORRUPTION AS PART OF THE NATIONAL ETHOS

Lanre Adewole reported in The NIGERIAN TRIBUNE edition of August 5, 2008 on how government officials collected twenty two million naira (N22m) bribe from job applicants during Immigration and the Prisons department recruitment efforts. Five (5) officials were subsequently arrested by the ICPC, one of the major crime fighting entities in the country.

According to the report;

"As investigation continues into the death of 43 applicants during recruitment tests conducted by two main agencies in the Ministry of Interior, the Independent Corrupt Practices and Other Related Offences Commission on Monday in Abuja revealed how a syndicate in the ministry collected over N22 million bribes from 140 applicants."

A statement from the commission and signed by its Spokes-person, Mr. Sina Babasola, disclosed that five members of the syndicate had been arrested and undergoing interrogation.

The statement read: "A special syndicate which specialises in demanding and collecting money from prospective applicants seeking employment into the Nigeria Prisons Service (NPS) and Nigeria Immigrations Service (NIS) has been smashed by operatives of the Independent Corrupt Practices and Other Related Offences Commission (ICPC). "The leader of the syndicate, a Chief Superintendent of Prison, Mrs. Mba Josephine Uchenna, attached to the Administration Department of the NPS, has been arrested by the commission in connection with the alleged scam."

To be accurate, the culture of corruption started taking roots a long time ago. It certainly was not helped by the types of leaders we've had, or a number of choices, we the citizens have made from time to time, even in our private lives.

I still recall that morning on July 17, 1986. Barely six weeks before I traveled to Canada on an academic scholarship for my Master of Laws (LL.M) RESEARCH PROGRAM.

I had just seen off my father who was heading abroad for another major surgery. I was not even certain I would ever see him alive again. Even then, I rued the turn of events that would require him to leave Nigeria's shores for an operation when I and the family would have preferred him to have it in Nigeria where we could visit and emotionally support him. But unfortunately, the hospitals had been (and continue to be) starved of resources and equipment by the nation's leadership. Which explains why President Yar'Adua feels obliged in 2008 (over two decades after my father's surgery) to proceed abroad in order to feel confident that he would be getting the appropriate medical attention! But I digress.

After stoically seeing off my father at the airport, I later went out for a quick take out breakfast with Yetunde who was then my girlfriend. So, this was (in the local parlance, very much during the 'AGO DIE' stage of the budding relationship) just prior to her promotion

I recall parking my recently purchased car across the street from the Donut and chicken place (I believe it was Chicken George fast food place which was then located just off Allen Avenue. This was **before Allen Avenue went to hell!**

This was before it was condemned to the hell of congestion and arbitrary rezoning, **turning it into a congested commercial bottle-neck**. The new Allen Avenue (like some similar places in Lagos) has become a far cry from its once serene, high brow and clean history. **A real example of backward progress!**

I had barely parked my car when a couple of vehicles swooped in, blocking me in and before I could bat an eye, they had chained my car to one of their towing vehicles. It was then I realized I have fallen victim to a syndicate of corrupt government workers (with the collusive blessing of some of their bosses, as I subsequently came to learn).

Legally, I had done nothing wrong! For years, everyone had used this side of the road for parking confidently recognizing that it was appropriate. Unfortunately, these were different times. The economy was in a downward swing and jobs were being lost right, left and center.

The cost of food was going up. So what was a syndicate of corrupt government employees to do but to further victimize its fellow citizens? AFTER ALL, THIS WAS THE AGE OF BABANGIDA AND THE ELEVATED CULTURE OF SETTLEMENT.

If the national leadership was taking its pound of flesh as part of its spoil for its successful military coup, the average government worker was also going to join in the national orgy.

So, my vehicle was illegally towed. I was thoroughly outraged and determined to fight this through the legal process. Alas, there was no legal process for redress. I found that out upon arrival at the area office which was just a few blocks away. I soon found out that this was an ongoing 'operation' to pad the wallets of government employees.

It turns out that this was another classic extortion scheme. They tow with the expectation of forcing you to "settle them (with a bribe) rather than pay the relatively stiffer penalty requiring the issuance of a receipt.

I initially thought that sanity might ultimately prevail when I saw one of their officials. He happened to be someone I had recently met by chance when we shared a Taxi ride and for whom I had done a favor and never thought I would ever have occasion to meet again. Good fortune right? Wrong!

I suppose he too was so suffused in the corrupt system with far too many of them beholden to its sustenance that the best he could offer me were platitudes.

Then it all came together. For weeks, I had worried about my Dad's impending surgery. At that very moment, he was in the air, flying to an uncertain surgical outcome.

Here was I confronted by the dregs of society whose preoccupation paled into insignificance when compared to the larger issues of life and death and the welfare of a beloved father.

And then the specter of a shifty eyed ingrate I had recently helped colluding at my expense with his cohorts, fleecing their fellow citizens under the color of office.

At that very moment, it all came together. And I shed tears for Nigeria.

They won the battle by causing me to spend money I had no business throwing away (even though I could afford it). But I didn't give them the full satisfaction. While you could never trust receipts issued to you, even back then **(because in Nigeria there is almost always 'official' and 'unofficial' receipts)**, I nevertheless elected to pay into the government coffers (for all the good that does) and insisted on collecting an 'official' receipt.

This was my rather tame but defiant victory, even as I walked away, shaken by the obscenity of this festering sore of corruption as part of our national ethos. These entrenched seedlings of open corruption and the culture of settlement were being systematically planted into the national consciousness well over two decades ago.

ALAS, THE GARDEN IS NOW INUNDATED WITH TERRIBLE OVERGROWTHS. IT IS CHOCKING THE LIFE OUT OF OUR FEW REMAINING BEAUTIFUL ROSES!

Considering the level of open and unapologetic corruption we have today, you could say that the 1980s were by comparison the good old days!

(b) POSTSCRIPT—THE TEARS LINGER STILL . . .

Over the past decade or so, I have traveled to Nigeria and spent extended time at least once each year. During a couple of the most recent trips, I could not help myself as the tears, though uninvited, nevertheless welled up as the plane touched down at the Muritala Mohammed International Airport in Lagos.

The eyes glistened and became misty as I beheld the predictably DARK SILHOUETTE OF THE ELECTRICITY DEPRIVED CITY OF

LAGOS (NO THANKS TO NEPA/ NATIONAL POWER HOLDING COMPANY). Nothing new there.

The tears began to dribble down slowly as I beheld the dust encrusted carcasses of vandalized and cannibalized long abandoned and now defunct Nigeria Airways planes littering the Airport grounds.

As we taxied toward the terminal, the tears fell. And they fell some more as I saw giant and unkempt weeds expanding their reach and vying for runway space as the planes fortunate height thankfully assisted in avoiding for the moment, the seeming inevitable confrontation with the weeds and shrubs determined to soar as nature would allow.

I blew my nose and wiped even more tears in readiness as the plane slowly approached its docking port, just meters away from frazzled Airport Touts, corrupt immigration and Customs Officers who, like dispassionate vultures had patiently awaited our arrival at the only available exit for the public.

Yes more tears rolled when I recalled how nice, clean and promising the atmosphere of the airport was barely three decades earlier when it was first opened. And how, over time, corruption, neglect and lack of foresight have all conspired to leave things as they are; a grimy crudely run low class and unnerving environment and a very (accurate but) uninspiring first impression of the country for first time visitors from abroad.

The tears flourished and cascaded even more as I reflected on how the Airport could have been better managed, expanded and modernized thereby creating more jobs and business opportunities for enterprising Nigerians.

Even away from these depressing images, when from time to time I recall or reflect on these realities, including the continuing wretched socio-economic existence of many of the people I regularly come across in Ekiti State, especially during my 2007 Campaign visit to many of the communities in Ekiti State, I still cannot help myself sometime but shed a few tears for the innocent people who ultimately bear the painful burden of corruption and a cynical oligarchy.

Alas, even as I force myself to share some of these hopeful cogitations in light of the Nation's many missed opportunities, not surprisingly, those tears linger still . . .

(c) ETHNICITY / RACE AS THE STRAWMAN FOR FAILED POLICIES

"North benefits little from oil wealth"—Maitama Sule

This report was culled from the August 5, 2008 edition of THIS DAY publication prepared by Ibrahim Shuaibu who was reporting from Kano, Nigeria.

According to the report;

"Former Nigerian Permanent Representative to the United Nation, Alhaji Maitama Sule, had declared that the north has "benefited little," from the country's oil wealth, ever since petrol became the main revenue earner.

Maitama Sule, who is the traditional title holder of Danmasanin Kano, said this during an interactive (exchange) with the minister of Energy (Gas), Chief Emmanuel Olatunde Odusina, on the Nigerian Gas Master Plan in Kano, which drew wild applause from northern stakeholders in attendance.

He said he wondered if such discriminatory action by successive governments in the country is not deliberate."

"I was the first Nigerian minister of Oil, Pa Ribadu and I were around when oil was discovered in 1957, we thwarted attempt to swindle the country, introduced competition in the sector, made selfless sacrifices, but today, the north has benefited little from oil wealth, I hope the action was not deliberate," Maitama Sule said.

On the implication of the rhetoric regarding an anti-north attitude by the Nation's leaders, never mind that apart from Obsanjo's brief interludes, all those who have really led Nigeria have been northerners!!!

Further, assuming Maitama Sule was right; it will only confirm what other Nigerians have experienced from successive corrupt and self-dealing leaders.

While they grow obscenely rich, the average citizen, whether in the north, east, south, west or Midwest have been mostly excluded from enjoying the natural blessings of this Nation.

NOW TO THE MOST PAINFUL PART OF THE REPORT;

According to Maitama Sule, a UN Report in 1962 listed Brazil, India and Nigeria as emerging industrialized nations, explaining that while Others had since achieved technological breakthrough, Nigeria still wallows in confusion.

He noted that; "It is so pathetic that while Brazil and India had achieved cognate technological breakthrough over the years, it is, however, painful that the Nigeria owned Defense Corporation set up to launch the country on the industrial path now produces furniture."

He said the oil wealth introduced a "negative culture of extravagance," adding that it has become a past time for Nigerian money bags today to bankroll frivolous overseas trips for mistresses and expressed optimism that the country can still get it right, going by the commitment demonstrated by the present regime to harness the abandoned natural gas for desired industrial growth."

JUST THINK FOR A MOMENT ABOUT WHAT MAITAMA SULE SAID ABOUT THE RELATIVE STAGNATION OF NIGERIA RELATIVE TO INDIA AND BRAZIL. LET IT MARINATE. HOPEFULLY, YOU'LL BE APPROPRIATELY OUTRAGED AND HOPEFULLY MORE DETERMINED TO WORK TOWARDS TRUE REPRESENTATIVE DEMOCRACY WHERE LEADERS ARE ACTUALLY ELECTED AND THUS MADE ACCOUNTABLE TO THE PEOPLE WITH RESPECT TO WHERE WE ARE AND HOW URGENTLY WE NOW NEED TO BE PROPERLY LED BY COMPETENT AND INSPIRED LEADERS!!!

It seems to me that when it comes to Africa and the blighted African American communities in the USA, I guess the more things seem to change the more they in fact stay the same.

For example, in the USA, The 'New Detroit' which I happily joined others in working hard to accomplish sadly reverted back (before it took hold) to the SAME OLD DETROIT, with the advent of a tyro (and for a while, the earring adorning geo-political neophyte) like **Kwame Kilpatrick** and his ilk.

Just another example of false promises of a better tomorrow ('RIGHT HERE, RIGHT NOW') made to Africans (and African Americans) and the community's penchant (WITH THE AID OF SOME SELF-SERVING RELIGIOUS LEADERS) to settle for platitudes, mediocrity and fast talking self-serving MESSIAHS of the current version of CHANGE (whatever that means)!

Graying, rusted, almost lifeless, groping, hoping
Your old paved streets are strewn with cracks
Peddlers entice your children to crack
Wisecracks at your expense, what a flak
Cynics abound to make a case and create a flak
Yet, you remain poised, searching, hoping, groping

Once ponderous and mightily subdued and grey
But BRIEFLY you came aglow and the twinkle was back
The bounce was back in the balls painted black
the cynics retreated en-mass
With identities revealed through the mask
Hiding, feigning, feinting, waiting again to prey

Once we beheld the majesty of the renaissance at night
What a sight
From the revolving summit
Folks Came and watched our people submit
To the splendor and luxury that was home grown in Detroit
Cruising through the tunnel, 'strait' to Detroit
Sipping on gin and juice as the rap song suggested

And rather briefly,
We felt our city was back
WE THOUGHT THE PAST WAS BEHIND US
WE THOUGHT WRONG!
WE HAD HOPED YOU WOULD COME WITH US
BUT it's NO LONGER safe again to sail
To Windsor, and the fox on Woodward at night
For in the current Detroit at night
Even the previously defeated Devil has sadly regained its knight

IMAGINE THAT! DETROIT, MISMANAGED AS A VERITABLE
THIRD WORLD ENCLAVE, RIGHT IN MIDDLE AMERICA!

WHETHER IN AFRICA OR BLACK AMERICA

Anybody who has not participated in the national orgy of corruption,
money laundering and kick backs and yet disputes the allegation that the
political class has been more of a costly and self serving group of leeches
than constructive contributors to the national development should answer
the following basic question;

**ARE YOU PERSONALLY BETTER OFF TODAY THAN YOU WERE
FOUR, EIGHT, SEVENTEEN OR EVEN THIRTY YEARS AGO?**

For much of post independence life in Nigeria, the country has mostly
drifted. Hampered by corrupt and inept leaders, harassed and undermined

by greedy foreign interests and allowed to drift by scared and generally emasculated population that desires the good life but is too afraid to believe it could achieve it. So, consistently, it fails at critical times to fight for it!

Yes indeed, to paraphrase the words of Malcolm X, we are the ones led astray. We have been run amok. We have been bamboozled. Our people have mostly been asleep at the wheel. It's time we awoke from this expensive stupor!

The country's fortune is almost analogous to the way many treat their relatives. Abandoned while alive, but feted and feasted upon in death!

The loved ones will play their part
Many self selected mourners
Will do their job with passion
Even some belching praise singers
Might be inspired
To sing the dirge
And to do it with soul and feeling
Alas, our dearly departed loved ones
Sleeping soul
Will remain undisturbed
From the eternal nest
That is installed

In the popularized tradition by **the comedian Stephen Colbert**, now is the time for a little **'wag of the finger'** to the **'fair weather friends,'** the secret back stabbers, the two-faced sell-outs, the glib liars and the spineless 'chicken-hawks' who do the disappearing act during battle but were always poised to make the grand appearance for CONTRACT SOLICITATION should you find yourself in office!

To be quite frank, these types of people are no more substantial than the shadow you need to ignore and never take seriously.

Yes
Shadow
You linger in the dark
And conveniently vanish
When your company is most desired
You make a formless phantom
Seem like a recalcitrant pest
When I cast about for you in desperation
To share my low moments
And be comforted by your reassuringly supportive presence
At difficult seasons that often hit me
Flush in the face
Like the burning sun unleashed
Designed to reveal my barely concealed insecurity
And self doubt
I have learned to persevere without your support
And in time, I am whole again
And soon enough
The time comes
And you sneak up beside me again
To share in my moments of glory
Away from the glare of the sun
That betrayed your true character
Oh, you sneaky phantom
You, the eternal fair weather friend
You, that lurks cynically in the dark
Picking your moments of contrived gallantry
A ploy rehearsed
To conceal your shame

Having experienced what we have, it really grates when we have to listen to some (citizens and other outsiders) tell us to settle for less. And they do this, even while they (or their communities) enjoy or take for granted what they would want us to deny ourselves. They need to settle down and put themselves in our shoes for a moment. I doubt they'll be comfortable walking a mile in those shoes!

If only you had walked a mile
In my favorite pair of shoes
When they were still new and snug
When the fit was good
Even the sole felt good

If only you had seen me walk a mile
In my favorite pair of shoes
As I stood tall and proud
When the shine glistened in the sun
And the soles applaud each stride with pride

If only there were any miles left to walk
In my favorite pair of shoes
But the shoes now seem broken and frail
And the skin is thinning and cracked
Even the soles are bruised and worn with age

Alas, there may not be much left
In my favorite pair of shoes
Even as the wear of age is showing
But the legacy of all the giant strides we took
Remain indelible and bold
Even on the shifting sands of time

Now, before the many rigged elections and fraudulent Census; before the self-serving coups; before Babangida, Abacha and Obasanjo; before the crooked civilian accomplices and the cynical foreign partners . . .

I remember happy days
When the din of laughter
And happy children
Fill each room with glorious sunshine
I remember quiet nights
When tired eyelids resist the urging of the night
Resistant still, even as the clock runs out
On another well-lived day
I remember the guttural belching of contented old ladies

The days of snow white rice and turkey legs
And the hunger inspiring chorus line
As our women folk enhance the yam
In tune with the mortar and pestle
I remember simpler times
When your word was truly your weight
The days when hope was real
And the joy of a neighbor on your account
Was truly earned and well deserved
I remember the days indeed
When true giants walked the earth
And sure-footed leaders led the way
Through thick shrubs and deep valleys
Over mountains, to the very heights
Of a people's exalted destiny
I remember
I remember, I say
Though the lights may fade and the horizon seem distant
Yet, I remember my duty to remember
And to happily remember
Remains my duty still

THE QUESTION IS DO YOU REMEMBER HOW IT WAS, OR HOW IT COULD STILL BE REDEEMED AND RENEWED?

ALAS, AFRICA REMAINS POISED AT THE EDGE OF PERMANENT PURGATORY

But then,
How did it come to this?
Why are WE in this place?
Chilled with desolation
The darkness is thick with uncertainty
The weight of this eerie fog exhausts even as one strives to exult
ARE WE here to be cleansed
Of all that shackles and ails OUR spirit

ARE WE to be teased and challenged by life's convoluted intrigues?
Or ARE WE indeed here to be submerged
And to be sunk into the very depths of ominous despair
ARE WE destined in time to partake of life's exhilaration?
And to soar with the thrill that attends inevitable reprieve?
ARE WE here to, in time behold and bask
In the majesty of the rainbow
As it hatches even from the womb of human despair to glorify the heavens
and illuminate troubled souls?
How did it come to this?
Why are WE in this place?
This desolate milieu for those that crave hope
This leveling desert for those thirsting for a leg up
Alas, are WE perchance here to be one of these lost souls
That have been consigned to call this chilling place home?
How did it come to this?
Pray tell, why are WE in this place?

So, the next practical or philosophical question is WHY?

Why does fate bless some
With abundance and beauty
And leave others bereft of hope and appeal
Yet, like the reddish Rose that flowers with appeal
Even the blessed are cursed with thorns in their beauty
Oh ye world, not so rounded, not so perfect and wholesome
Why do birds choose to sing
To delight tone-deaf trees
And the ugly larvae grows to become a beautiful butterfly
Only to glorify arid seasons and feast on lowly flies
Yet, many dynamic souls are grounded to the earth like trees unable to soar
with the birds that sing
Why spend an eon laboring to mount the crest
Only to get to the summit and be challenged to conquer the next
And in a whimsical moment tear to shreds
What was carefully woven with iron threads
Belatedly, we make the best quest of life the next
Even as the zeal to surmount the rest begins to crest
Why?

We should therefore be focused on the practical and the pragmatic. For example, what do we do next to get us back on the right track.

The defiant Wole Soyinka and the irrepressible Gani Fawehinmi are now in their seventies. Gani especially is currently struggling with major health issues and my fervent prayers are with him and his family. God willing, these two giants (and others of their stature) will still be around for many more years to come so they could regale us with their wisdom and patriotic fervor.

But, just like for all of us, time is running out. It is time to have the torch being passed to the next generation of credible and deserving patriots handled with some focus and grit.

Before the 2007 elections, in fact as early as 2005, I wrote and implored progressive forces in Nigeria to jettison personal ambition and to coalesce around one political party and muster all the progressive forces to win political power without the heavy weights battling each other and weakening the movement by diluting the power of a strong coalition.

I published this initiative on the web and also personally arranged for the delivery of copies to some of the usual movers and shakers. I don't mind confessing that I was and remain very disappointed that these leaders did not make a better effort of uniting their forces in order to win power away from the corrupt and ineffectual administration of Obasanjo.

Who cares whether the President is a Yoruba, Igbo or Hausa when we cannot even guarantee uninterrupted power for any city in Nigeria, and yet we wonder why Nigeria is yet to unleash its potential for an industrial revolution!

FURTHER, WE MUST BE PREPARED TO DEFY KIRIKIRI
-Their Cynical Ace in the Hole

Kirikiri, now the finishing school
For irrepressible poet to brood or possibly to waste away
Or perchance to cobble together more stinging prose
Dispatched discreetly by retail

Let's echo the verses cobbled at our respective (metaphorical) Kirikiri
Let it spell defiance
Even as we set our spirits free
From the shackles of fear and uncertainty

THEY'VE DONE THEIR WORSE. WHAT ELSE
CAN THEY STEAL OR INFLICT ON US THAT THEY HAVEN'T
ALREADY?

**FOR ALL OUR COLLECTIVE INTELLECTUAL ACUMEN, I MUST
RESPECTFULLY CONFESS THAT, BASED ON THE FORTY PLUS
YEAR TRACK RECORD, MY COLLEAGUES IN THE PROGRESSIVE
MOVEMENT STILL HAVE MUCH TO LEARN ABOUT THE
EFFECTIVE ACQUISITION, EXERCISE AND MAINTENANCE
OF POLITICAL AUTHORITY—THE MOST ELEMENTARY
DEFINITION OF DEMOCRATIC POLITICS!**

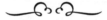

**"Bad fortune is what good fortune leans on; good fortune is what bad
fortune hides in"—Wisdom of the TAO**

4.

AFRICAN DEMO-KRAZY

—A BRIEF MOMENT OF CLARITY

(1)

LET'S OPEN WITH A LITTLE BIT OF IRONY.

Wednesday June 9, 2004 (right as our so-called nascent democracy was entering its second term), Assistant Commissioner Dan Odiah, obviously following the instructions of his superiors, led a team of police officers numbering up to 500 (without regard to the right to peaceful assembly and freedom of expression), to storm an event organized to mark the annulment of the June 12, 1993 elections by the military oligarchy.

The police officers used tear gas, sealed up the secretariat of the Nigerian Union of Journalists and arrested a few of the attendees.

The Oshogbo event was organized by Mrs. Teju Abiola (one of the widows of CHIEF MKO Abiola, THE WINNER OF THE ANNULLED ELECTIONS). Mrs. Teju was also reportedly detained for a while as a consequence of the incident.

Obasanjo was the beneficiary of years of agitation against Babangia and Abacha for the actualization of the June 12 1993 election results.

So the irony is rather palpable that the beneficiary of our struggles would head a government committed to suppressing legitimate conversations and recognition of that seminal moment in the country's history.

Rather too often, in Nigeria especially, the wicked have tended to come out on top at the expense of the virtuous and the meritorious. One could only hope that the tide is slowly beginning to turn. But, we'll see.

(2)

Sometime toward the end of May in 2004, then National Chairman of the ruling PDP, Chief Audu Ogbeh OPENLY BLAMED "supposed leaders" FOR THE SPATE OF ASSASSINATIONS ROCKING THE COUNTRY.

Echoing a similar sense of frustration and seeming helplessness verbalized by other dignitaries at the event (which included Governor Peter Odili), Ogbeh wondered aloud "why is it so difficult for us to tolerate different opinions and accommodate our differences?"

For one thing, it wasn't then (and it certainly isn't even now) the least reassuring to hear those in charge of the country and all of the paramilitary forces throw up their hands helplessly in frustration.

Further, it begs the question whom 'the supposed leaders' Ogbeh was referring to, considering that he, Obasanjo and their party pretty much represented the effective leadership of the country.

(3)

One of the things many Nigerians (especially a number of our politicians) live for is the ability to have access to what the COMMON PEOPLE don't (like the ability to travel abroad to 'rest;' 'for medical checkup' or pretty much to enjoy a "civilized" environment.

Never mind the (national) self esteem issues this raises, or the irony that many of these folks are (or were) in charge of the country and could thus make (or have made) it as pleasant, as 'civilized' and nice a place as any to 'rest' or secure 'medical checkup.'

So, it's been quite frustrating for a number of current and former leaders who have not been able to enjoy one of this natural perks (having been precluded from traveling to the United States, for example).

Actually, this has been especially inconvenient particularly for some of the recent Governors caught up in the EFCC investigation, since United States and the UK used to be the favored spots where a number of our corrupt leaders prefer to hide their stolen loot.

(4)

Abacha's reign was brutish, nasty and long. He presided over massive corruption. Even his children had to be forced to reluctantly disgorge some of the illegally obtained funds belonging to the country.

For example, on April 17, 2005, Abba, Abacha's second son was flown out to face money laundering charges in Switzerland. He had been arrested in Germany where he was attempting to close another account where he was the sole signatory.

And so the hide and seek game continued, with stolen monies that were hidden all over the world were being tracked, including those hidden in water tanks specially built to hold millions at bay while millions of citizen starve.

And given the pedigree of the Obasanjo administration, rather than be forceful and outraged in the disgorgement efforts, we saw the regime NEGOTIATE A SETTLEMENT OF SORTS with the Abacha family rather than give them an ultimatum including appropriate jail terms for being active Participants in the corruption enterprise (both pre and post Abacha's demise).

Not only did the nation endure this, but recently people had to listen (with increasing lassitude) as Babangida and Abdulsalam tried their hands at revisionist history by seeking to white-wash the Abacha years and his sordid legacy.

It is not too surprising that these two former heads of state (who themselves are in need of rehabilitation) would attempt this. The real irony is that if Nigeria were a society governed by the rule of law, neither man would be currently free much less have the national media platform from whence they could from time to time pontificate.

THE MYTH OF THE ANARCHIST
(and a few of the cynically defined "Terrorist" Groups)

Whenever a people rise up with passion
In seeming response to the exhortation
Of an inspirational idealist
It does so
Only because it was emotionally
And ideologically
Ripe for the pickings
It would have found another reason to rise
Even in the absence of the compelling eloquence
Of a tiresome idealist
Indeed, it only needed the inspirational catalyst
That the ideas themselves represent
If people are not dissatisfied,
Disillusioned or disdainful
Or prone to revolt
Millions of provocative statements may be made
Even by the most powerful of orators
And they would not have the slightest effect
Indeed, the powerfully elegant words would fall
Lamely and without pageantry
As would a hapless fluttering dew would impress

On an impervious concrete slab
But if the reverse were the case
Then, even without the oratorical flourish
Of an advocating potentate in waiting,
The population would eventually seize
On whatever excuse there is
To rise in rebellion
If their deficient circumstances
Made it inevitable

From Illusory Independence DAY; To Pointless Election DAY; To Fedeco/
Inec Result Manipulation DAY; To June 12 Aborted Democracy Day; To
Obasanjo's Military Demo-Krazy DAY . . .

EACH OF WHICH (in its own right) is truly A MOST UNINSPIRED
DAY

The proud Hibiscus
Shrivels and pouts
In the wake
Of a diffuse
And indifferent
Early morning glare
Of a dull autumn day
And with retracted petals
The flowery peacocks
Flop in unison
To rebel
Against the gloom
Of a most
Uninspired day

WITH A PATTERN SO ODIOUS AND UNINSPIRING, ISN'T IT
ABOUT TIME WE DREW A LINE IN THE SAND AND INSISTED
ENOUGH WAS ENOUGH?

WHAT ARE YOU INSPIRED BY?
TEMPORAL MATERIAL GAINS?
ENDURING LEGACY OF GOOD WORKS?

Either way, MAMA AFRICA BECKONS . . .

HOME
Beyond the trees
And all the shrubs that have turned brown
Beyond vast fields
With graying foliage and the trees' raised brow
Is a place longed for
A place called HOME in summer or fall

Where laughter rings true
And the warmth seeps through
Where the joy is full
And every stomach too
Where families chatter
And little children matter

HOME
That happy place
Where families live and friends converge
Though dreams diverge even as we converge
Happy still is that place
That happy place called HOME

However, beyond this sentimental longing, is a zone of pragmatism and reality. On the one hand, you have the foreboding PYRHIC VICTORY and seeming inevitability of a physical demise where death's triumph is accomplished over the physical body. On the other, you have a chance at double immortality through an enduring positive legacy, long after you shed your current physical manifestation.

FIRST, WE MUST OVERCOME THE 'SAME OLD-SAME OLD'

Let me be clear. There are plenty of good people in politics, whether in Nigeria or America; plenty of good people, irrespective of political affiliations. However, there are equally many who, limited by unconquered desires CHOOSE to cynically promote rather ephemeral self serving agendas AT THE EXPENSE OF THE COMMON GOOD.

Further, these good folks in politics have an obligation to let their glorious lights shine!

Without making waves for positive change, merely being good is no longer good enough. **Each must play a role in "disturbing and unsettling the current unjust peace."**

Certainly in a world where far too many miss out on the promise of the 'good life', we have no business coddling ineffectual leaders, even if they are cute, are of the same ethnic group or race as we are.

We must call them on it lest we keep moving in circles and watch helplessly as potentially great communities whether in Africa or the United States are led into chaos and perdition by self-serving and ineffectual leaders.

FORMER MAYOR KWAME KILPATRICK OF DETROIT (WHO HAPPENS TO BE AFRICAN AMERICAN) IS A CASE IN POINT. OLUSEGUN OBASANJO AND IBRAHIM BABANGIDA, TWO FORMER PRESIDENTS OF NIGERIA REPRESENT ANOTHER SET OF PERFIDIOUS EXAMPLES.

I guess it's true what they say. The more things change the more they stay the same. The new Detroit sadly reverted back to the OLD Detroit, with the advent of a tyro (and for a while, the ear-ring adorning geo-political neophyte) like **Kwame Kilpatrick** and his ilk. Just another example of false promises of a better tomorrow ('RIGHT HERE, RIGHT NOW') made to **Africans (and African Americans)** and the community's penchant to settle for platitudes, mediocrity and fast talking self-serving MESSIAHS of the current version of CHANGE (whatever that means)!

Folks Came and watched our people submit
To the splendor and luxury that was home grown in Detroit
Cruising through the tunnel, 'strait' to Detroit
Sipping on gin and juice as the rap song suggested
And rather briefly,
We felt our city was back
WE THOUGHT THE PAST WAS BEHIND US
WE THOUGHT WRONG!
WE HAD HOPED YOU WOULD COME WITH US
BUT it's NO LONGER safe again to sail
To Windsor, and the fox on Woodward at night
For in the current Detroit at night
Even the previously defeated Devil has regained its knight

IMAGINE THAT. DETROIT, MISMANAGED AS A VERITABLE THIRD WORLD ENCLAVE, RIGHT IN MIDDLE AMERICA!

—ₘₒₒₑₓₒₒₓₑₒₒₘ—

BILL COSBY BLOWS UP!

—ₘₒₒₑₓₒₒₓₑₒₒₘ—

Bill Cosby (A RENOWNED AFRICAN AMERICAN ENTERTAINER, EDUCATOR AND PHILANHROPIST) tried to raise some of these similar concerns in a different context when he spoke up in 2004 about the CRISIS IN THE AFRICAN AMERICAN COMMUNITY; the negative gap in educational achievements, poor parenting, high rate of out of wedlock births (babies having babies), low expectations, rampant drug abuse and higher crime rates as compared to other ethnic groups or communities in the United States.

This dangerous downward spiral of the next generation of African Americans continues to raise concerns. However, Cosby has also received a lot of criticism, not so much that he was substantially off the mark, but because of his TONE!

While I may not be in complete agreement with Bill Cosby, **I agree with his sense of urgency and the need for some internal accountability in the various African American communities (including the legion of churches and church leaders who never relent in raising and replenishing their 'building funds,' but spend less time doing real and meaningful community outreach to serve those in need of support and inspiration in their often blighted communities.**

THE MILITARY FRANCHISE (REVISITED)

Alas, in Nigeria, the more things seem to be poised for positive change, the more they sadly remain the same (or worse!). This vicious cycle of hard luck, hard knocks and hard times is due in large measure to revisionists, entrenched military interests, their civilian cohorts, media apologists and many beneficiaries and co-conspirators in the private sector, including those who help them hide and launder their stolen loot. Here is to hoping that you all choke on this!

SO AGAIN TO MY COMPATRIOTS-
LET US REFLECT AND REASON TOGETHER

Follow Your Mind

Like prior initiatives, this effort is both a historical analysis and a brief political commentary on Africa, and specifically on the Nigerian experience. It is a labor of love.

I am motivated to write this NEW Book (and to stay the progressive course) because I desire to share a few ideas that burn within. And hopefully to challenge the seemingly sanguine attitudes of our people towards institutionalized political domination and economic oppression.

After all, being relatively young independent nations, we must set the feet of these new African nations on the path of knowledge because through knowledge comes strength. And the more exposures to new ideas, and recycled old ones, the faster would our infantile and rather rudimentary geopolitical structures grow.

The current leadership in most African Countries may resent the fact of having the issues dealt with in this book so bluntly addressed, but we should not be intimidated thereby.

It is no treason (OR TERRORISM) to desire freedom. **The goal of this book (AND ALL MY RELATED INITIATIVES), it should become clear, if it isn't already, is to follow the inspired and inspiring traditions of those true heroes that have gone before us who were genuinely driven by a commitment to bring our people out from under the bitter bondage of slavery; colonialism; more recently military dictatorship and the degrading dilemma of an arrested democracy.**

Things have gotten so bad, and we know it. In a desperate bid, we cast about for reassurance and even contemplate mythical messages in the sky (often to the delight of preying cynical religious merchants of doubtful faith or conviction). But we strain in vain. **Even old and familiar sounds that use to reassure now chill our dank and humid nights with its cold contempt.**

Yes, like millions of other citizens, **I love AFRICA and indeed this country called Nigeria; the land of my birth. The place I was suckled on my mother's milk.**

But my love for it has not blinded me to the festering sore that begins to eat deep into its very foundations, for even love cannot drown truth.

As individuals, we all must follow different paths. In fact those who love this country of mine and for that matter the African Continent as passionately as I do may consciously or unconsciously elect to employ less cerebral means of demonstrating that love and particular concern for its yet unfulfilled promise.

Personally, I feel compelled by a resolve from deep within, to set my feet upon this course that I have always known I must follow.

For years, ours has been a legacy of political bondage and servitude without rest; an inefficacious economic toil without just reward.

The lack of good leadership has dulled our commitment, and misapplied quota system in the distribution of deserts has dampened our sense of amity and community.

Therefore, if our people seem burdened, it is from the weight of oppression; if they appear physically and psychologically bruised, it is from the jab of injustice from an undeserving leadership whose lack of grace and imagination is so great, it gives credibility to the silly notion that perhaps the Sahara desert's heat has melted their reason under its intense scrutiny.

We have languished for so long under the verbal lash and the condescending conceit of willful taskmasters who are always ready to whip us into conformity by the sheer force of their whimsical inclinations. But we have confounded them with our staying power.

They probably have long expected us to cry out for the mercy of death as an escape from our servitude, recognizing that when a destitute dies, he only loses the pain of living.

But, in a manner reminiscent of slap-happy killjoys, we persevered. What many of these people inflicted on us, they did willingly and cynically. They were invested with positions of trust, but instead, they were found in the midst of treachery and treason.

Indeed, it is the height of mindless callousness and arrogance that make men like these turn their fellow humans into manipulable pawns and replaceable beasts of burden. It may yet be meet to unleash the vengeful dogs of hell as they continue to be wickedly unrepentant and remain in the shadow of our collective wrath.

However, in Nigeria, military coups and counter-coups, we now realize are not helpful to our political and economic growth. Thanks to Idiagbon and Buhari, the discredited Nigerian politicians left in a cloud of dust and disgrace. Alas, they have since returned with flourish and fanfare in a blaze of glory. Where hath our redeemer gone?

The hope is that with a new breed of leadership, the transition to a Truly elected civilian government will eventually lead to a new dawn of economic sanity; political sobriety and social stability.

The darkness of oppression and ineptitude will at some point pass over us with the inevitable changing of the guard. Thereafter, the light of freedom would shine over our peoples. But first, we must stun our leaders with a jolt of reality.

They must be invited to descend from their arrogant carriage and awake from their delusions of grandeur. It is indeed a strange system of public service when the minister becomes the one being ministered unto.

This country called Nigeria, like several other countries in Africa was established as a post colonial republic over four decades ago, longer than the average life expectancy in some communities.

Previously, we could have laid claim to several alibis, including the view that for much of our formative years, we were limited by the horizon of youth. Now, we have to get on with making the bold new changes needed to usher in the new dawn of hope that we have all longed for and eminently deserve.

The past atrocities of our leaders (both military and civilian) have shamed us. We must let that season of infamy remain in the past where it belongs. Let us quietly sink it into silence, and for the future, let us watch out for the cynical revisionists who reside at the heels of a new promising dawn aiming to abort the birth of fair play and good government for the citizens of Africa.

Being merely imbued with an aloof carriage does not a leader, make. The key to efficient teamwork is a leadership that inspires loyalty, because it shares in our pain and actually understands our every yearning. The leadership must also command respect by sheer force of character, not the coercive barrel of a gun.

If the follower-ship has confidence in the leadership, it would clearly reward it with increased productivity and an inevitable collective success. Without a doubt, a leader should be accessible, friendly, polite, and sincere, on top of the issues, lead by example, be fair and certainly be firm.

We should no longer encourage this delusions of grandeur that imbues public officials with big egos warranting their expectation that citizens should abide their every sick whim meekly and with total submission.

This silliness is an unfortunate carryover from our largely defunct colonial heritage.

We must move away from this denigration of human dignity. It certainly is a legacy not to be passed on to dampen the drive and stunt the valiant spirit of coming generations.

Incidentally, a major vestige of our sad legacy, especially in Nigeria is the daylight extortion that takes place openly and with impunity at the tout overrun Muritala Mohammed International Airport in Lagos with the obvious collusion of the Customs, Immigration, securities forces and their bosses.

In case word has not gotten out yet, they should know that thanks to their efforts, Nigeria (the so-called Giant of Africa) now has another reason to be the laughing stock around the civilized world.

All foreign airlines coming to Nigeria (grudgingly I might add) now warn their citizens who might be considering traveling to Nigeria of the lawlessness and shameful chaos and disorder at the airport. They now know, as we have all known for quite a while now that no luggage is safe.

Merely having a confirmed ticket with a boarding pass guarantees nothing. It certainly does not ensure that the often corrupt officials have not arbitrarily sold your seat to a higher bidder who was not even booked to fly on the plane!

The customs post, like other similar law enforcement posts around the country, are no more than toll gates where illicit money change hands. Alas, day light bribery has assumed an art form that is celebrated at the expense of hard-working law abiding citizens who are held hostage by obviously underpaid Officers intent on extracting their pound of flesh, unfortunately from other social victims like themselves.

Even the Nigerian Postal Service has refused to be out-hustled. The shenanigans by NIPOST employees are well documented. Unfamiliar with our very corrupt system, many foreigners were nonplussed that such infamy could be so openly perpetrated unchecked. But we know better.

The point is that these atrocities could not have taken root and festered without at least the tacit approval from the very top. The shame of this is that, with respect to the "airport show", a visitor coming to the Country for the first time is force-fed the very worse about us even before the visitor has the chance to learn about the Country's more endearing qualities.

Additionally, as a fiscal matter, these practices have effectively stalled the growth of commerce, destroyed the prospect for a lucrative and worthy tourist industry for the Country and generally given the country a dismal reputation.

Aside from the usual condescending propaganda, our unwholesome reputation around the world is now legendary. This is why most foreigners would not invest in our economy.

Honestly, we cannot blame them because even those who fed fat on the country's wealth have declined to reinvest part of that wealth back in our economy.

Instead, they have elected to put those monies in foreign accounts to help sustain the economies of communities that could never even see beyond our allegedly inferior skin color which is deemed the indisputable evidence of inferior intellect.

I guess these leaders of ours can't be very smart to have turned their backs on their own heritage. They are certain to eventually inherit the wind.

All the internal revenues that the government needs desperately to improve our infrastructure system and the policies designed to be employed in protecting local commerce against unfair foreign competition are lost or compromised on account of this greed and systemic graft.

Citizens should begin to put the Country first, if they really hope to get reprieve from this barrage of illegitimate fiscal, social and psychological burden. It is well known that most citizens, who are otherwise averse to it, bribe or allow themselves to be extorted so as not to be inconvenienced.

Unfortunately, this attitude is exactly what these official crooks are counting on when they make their tongue-in-cheek **"wetin u carry?"** (What do you have on you?), request.

If the reverse were the case, and most citizens instead refuse to bribe or be extorted by making a loud but peaceful rejection of the illegal request, this would at least begin to move the country towards the path of sanity and the rule of law.

It certainly would not make all our travails disappear overnight; nor will it put bread on most tables. However, stemming this egregious practice will enhance the quality of life in most of our cities while bolstering the government's coffers enough for it to give effect to some of its better policies that were designed to create a more just society.

The reality however is that, were the country's leadership so disposed, these atrocious and illegal practices could have been easily crushed and stamped out. Instead, like festering sores, they continue to expand and grow in scale. Consequently, like most of the other ills that afflict this nation (and other African Countries), it boils down to the primary thesis of this book.

A real change (for the better) in the caliber and quality of the nation's leadership is ultimately the singular most important break we can make with our inglorious past. Yes, you may quote this line. The primary solution (if indeed there is any) lies in the change of leadership!

SELECTIVE SUICIDE
(AS A WINDOW INTO RACIAL PRIDE AND SELF ESTEEM)

It was a snowy day. The wind was also strong. We had chosen an inauspicious time to go out shopping. The Weatherman's somber account proved prophetic. We had been cynical. We would not be talked out of taking advantage of a **special White sale at SEARS.**

We were not even sufficiently clad for the bitter winter weather. Health-wise, the situation was getting out of hand. We decided to take refuge in the BI-RITE store nearby. This was a tactical move to preserve life and limb.

The inclement weather persevered. We waited gratefully in the warm comfort of the store. We would purchase an article or two in appreciation of the warm hospitality.

Casually, we set about our purpose. We looked around the store with the arrogant carriage of people with an impressive purchasing power.

We had less than a hundred and fifty dollars between the three of us. The sum available for immediate expenditure was even far less. The store attendants fussed over us with practiced gusto. You almost felt they had a tip that we were the heirs-apparent to a self-proclaimed life president of a backward oil-rich Country.

The modesty of our financial situation remained our secret. We resolved not to blow our cover.

We noticed that the other customers were not commanding similar attention. You would reckon they must have been green with envy; except of course if we were merely under the close surveillance of the store detectives. I noticed the attention of an elderly man in a black bowler hat. I nodded in his direction to acknowledge his presence.

He responded with a scowl. But then, in retrospect, age seemed to have set his face into a permanent scowl. So when I grinned at him and he mumbled something that came across as an obscenity, I kindly reasoned that he probably was not feeling comfortable with his new dentures.

In the interim, the obsequious attendants must have been disappointed we did not mortgage our limbs for some of their more esoteric products. We went to the cashier and stood in line. We were determined not to be intimidated into putting an unwise dent on our limited resources. We looked everywhere but at the beseeching countenance of the attendant making a provocative sales pitch.

There was no time for expensive sentiments. The weather outside had improved in the interim. We could see the midday sun rising from the horizon. We concentrated hard on paying for the few items we had picked.

We were determined not to let some scantily dressed leggy attendant break our defenses. Gosh! How easily an assumed aloof resistance breaks down to pay homage to Man's primal animal instincts!

The mind continued to stray helplessly to consider the amorous uses those shapely legs could be put. Sensing weakness, the leggy attendant moved in for the kill.

Someone panted. Another familiar voice groaned with restrained ecstasy. My colleagues denied responsibility. Perhaps my ears were playing tricks with me. And I thought as you age, it is the memory that goes first.

My situation must have been unique. I had my eyes. My mind was also alert. My eyes caught the familiar figure of a man shunting impatiently in front of me. Both the conduct and the personality registered in my memory.

Images of tactical shunting for choice chicken parts and ice cream on Sunday afternoons at the former University of Ife (Nigeria) cafeteria brought back nostalgic memories of better times.

Unfortunately, the slow smile that was working its way back to my face was frozen in time and promptly disappeared as I beheld the sour personality planting him-self squarely across my path.

He was the elderly man in the black bowler hat. He was in his late sixties. He was now collecting his change at the check-out counter. I stood patiently in line behind him. I waited my turn.

Alex Adeyinka, one of my colleagues at the local university was with me. Kemi Odujirin, another colleague was also on hand. Kemi had just arrived from Nigeria with the usual wide-eyed expectancy of some-one new to this reputed land of milk and honey.

In spite of some initial disappointments, we made a point of emphasizing the humorous aspects of our situation in Canada. We were deep in one of the many fond reminiscences of our respectively eventful, even if checkered experiences at the then University of Ife.

While in Canada, we could barely make ends meet. Our paltry scholarship constituted the entire bulk of our respective incomes. However, anytime we got together, we somehow succeeded in having a good laugh. Never mind that for the most part, the joke was on us.

This was one of such occasions when the three of us were in relatively high spirits. During this period, I had, in a stereotypical fashion began to wonder why some of our Caucasian colleagues appear stiff and uptight.

From my limited interactions (at the time) with people from other cultures, I had come to identify subtle condescension with the British. A habit, I reasoned, they were having difficulty in shedding even long after they had ceased to rule the waves. Apparently, I concluded in my generalization flourish, that the British were not alone.

It was especially curious, however, that any time we appeared to be having a good time; we were met with puzzled glances as if to register both astonishment and frustration. There continues to be astonishment at our large capacity for forbearance and frustration at our incredible staying power as a race that will not disappear, despite Centuries of hate, oppression and malice.

In a comical way, it sort of reminds you of the recalcitrant Energizer Battery that would not quit. There we were again making waves when we were supposed to be quietly grateful for our rare privilege, and to discreetly go through each day as apologetic members of an inferior race.

No, the Ku Klux Klan and their ideological heirs will not care very much for our shameless exuberance at all. They have ravaged the homes and broken the bones of erstwhile slaves for far less misdemeanors. But we are a recalcitrant bunch, it would appear. We are seeking to graduate from apologetic Negroes, to defiantly self assured blacks.

Well, FOR A QUICK FLASH FORWARD. **Now comes Barack Obama and the so-called POST-PARTISAN GENERATION.** One can only hope Obama does well enough to keep these positive trends going, not just in the United States, but around the world.

In the meantime, many still cannot imagine a Black person in the White House! Afro-Americans my foot! The feeling was (and sadly still is) that, rather audaciously, these people, these former slaves are growing wings! Now, this is the background on our world, then and now.

The point, however, is that this patronizing attitude is not limited to the realms of politics. It rears its head daily in the various interactions between so-called Blacks and people of other races, whether in America, Canada, or in the Far East.

Even some Blacks from the Caribbean Island, imbued by the apparently intoxicating proximity to American technology and culture occasionally affect superiority to Africans living in North America. Someone should remind some of these simpletons from whence their Fathers came.

In some of these otherwise civilized societies, racism, whether subtle or overt is a way of life. Not many cities in either the United States or Canada can boast of a Police department that does not let racial stereotypes and suspicion dominate the mode of performing their constitutional duties.

I will not even bother to begin citing any of the legions of racially motivated incidents involving the police. The Rodney King buffeting by the white Los Angeles police officers was only unique because it is a recorded instance of a slew of similar daily occurrences.

The average citizen still has his or her own way of reflecting deeply held prejudices. For example, the average Caucasian in the southern part of the United States is not too bothered about how close to him the Black family lives (recall the proximity of the out-houses during the slavery years), as long as the Black individual does not ascend over him to a position of authority.

The self-styled liberal Yankees in the Northern sections of the Country tolerate the situation that allows for the possible economic success of the average Black person as long as the Black or other racial minority-does not attempt to socialize too closely with his "racial superiors"(?).

Apart from casual efforts at appearances, unfortunately, especially during the divisive Reagan and (Willie Horton) Bush years, the average blue collar Caucasian was probably more likely to be racist than not. This is partly because he or she is erroneously encouraged (sometimes overtly) to feel superior to people of other races.

Unfortunately for everyone, racism begets both activist and defensive racism. Apparently, with the election of Obama, it would seem that political expediency and ruling economic imperatives have forced some movement towards mutual toleration in some communities.

This is a faint cause for hope. However, until it is ultimately recognized that these erstwhile slaves will not simply burrow holes in the ground and disappear, tension will continue to reign, and the benefits of constructive cooperation stifled, and its rewards put in abeyance.

Meanwhile, at the store, the elderly man in the black bowler hat completed his transaction with the cashier. He swore and turned abruptly upon me. He regarded me coolly. He studied my features. Apparently, nothing unusual: Two legs and all. No tails visible.

We were both now at smelling distance of each other. I could tell it was definitely his closest encounter with a Black . . . (Whatever), and I was his specimen.

"Do you have a rope"? he inquired in a conspiratorial voice. I was elated. I reasoned that he must have liked what he saw. In my eagerness to help, I was almost being obsequious.

A Whiteman actually requested for my help! And he did it with impeccable English too! Apparently, I reckoned, he was crediting me with the ability to comprehend the language in its correct form. In retrospect, I wonder now if this perhaps was an impromptu skills test.

I should have known there was a trap somewhere. "No, I don't have a rope", I responded with sincere regrets. I was Sad because I could not be of help. However, I made a mental note of getting some ropes in case some other person should ask me next time.

Who knew whether it was a secret code, or for that matter the ultimate gesture that will finally ease me into the mainstream of their society; A luxury hither-to reserved only for those who help marry their army of homely 'lovelies'

Not to appear unenthusiastic to help, I anxiously asked the elderly man what he wanted a rope for, in case I could come up with an alternative idea of how to satisfy his immediate need.

I probably should have kept my nose away from his sanctimoniously white task. I should not have fussed too much in deference to his advanced age as if it was my fault that death was imminently upon him.

In any event, he responded to my inquiry by triumphantly confessing to me that he was merely wondering whether my friends and I could lay our hands on enough ropes to go mercifully hang ourselves. His facade of elderly fragility was no longer in place. He had suddenly come upon an obvious cause to live for.

The grotesque image of us three hanging lifelessly from a post must have given his pitiful life some new impetus. It appeared that from the excitement and rage contorting his face into an almost adorable sneer, he had finally stumbled upon his life's calling as a jingoistic zealot.

He directed vicious diatribes and racial innuendoes at us. He was taking no prisoners. We were initially taken aback by the unexpected vituperations, and the open campaign of orchestrated polemics he was seeking to wage.

Didn't they bring Christian brotherhood to us pagans, until the issue turned on an acknowledgment of equality? Well, it did not matter. I was quick at the draw. He was surprised that we did not feel intimidated by all the white folks around us. We three were the only Blacks in the Store.

We were grossly out-numbered if push came to shove. It was evident that many of the people were still having trouble adjusting to not seeing us Black folks in shackles and chains. It was their Country. It was their Store. We had no business disturbing their peace with our offensively happy presence.

More importantly, though, we seized the opportunity to rise to the defense of our race. In the face of adversity, one's sense of personal preservation could be very keen. We were not apologetic. We were not going to hang ourselves. We refused to make their day.

He walked away fuming. We did too. However, the issues will not go away. They must be confronted. But first, we must keep our own house in order. This effort, therefore, is symbolic of the urgent itch that can no longer be ignored.

Many of us in Africa have remained at best; cautiously optimistic in view of the infamy we have had to contend with in our respective societies.

We have witnessed set-backs and frustrations at one time or another. And not all our (National) dreams will come true in our own lifetime.

Even some otherwise routine goals occasionally take some doing to achieve. But we must never relent. We must always persevere because through adversity comes strength.

In retrospect, one cogitated that the cantankerous racist we encountered may have had a gun. Many of them do. He may have shot to kill. He may then be exculpated by their civilized justice system that is not altogether above pandering to constituency prejudices. Retro-actively, he could be found to be mentally ill.

He would therefore not be held responsible for his actions. And if you should inquire off the record from either the Florida, the Los Angeles' Sergeant Koon, Mark Fuhrman and their ilk, or for that matter, from the Montreal police department, whether Blacks were expendable, you might be embarrassed by a rare display of human candor.

Even the Nigerian embassy, (like some other so-called third world countries) based on its track record will probably merely weave and bob at the fringes.

Such events must not be allowed to interfere with the generous transfer of technology from our friends, the government officials would argue, rather than stand up for the integrity of a victimized citizen. They would conclude that the Whiteman is too civilized to kill without being appropriately provoked. Excuse us for living!

In any case, some would wonder why we did not stay at home to help salvage the battered economy by helping to swell the unemployment lines. Others would dismiss accounts of our deaths as either blatant rumors, or definitely drug related. What can I tell you? We are a cynical lot

On the streets of Lagos, some of those who ordinarily prefer to be killed by a "JEEP" or a Mercedes Benz, rather than by a battered Volkswagen, or a Russian Lada, would be envious of the manner of our deaths. I am certain some are still grudging Dele Giwa, the murdered editor-in-chief of Newswatch Magazine, for his triumphant exit (going as he did in what was then an unprecedented noisy blaze of explosives).

They may even fantasize their own romantic deaths in the precious hands of a Whiteman. The crazier the better! Had we been killed in the hands of the intolerant white man who would rather see us hang, or others like him, some of our sick brethren with major self esteem problems would have willingly traded places with us!

This is a pitiful testament to the deplorable state of our national psyche, especially in Nigeria, and conceivably in some other parts of the so-called third world. Thanks to the well chosen foreign television programs, our children can now easily aspire to play "White".

Thanks to the convenient summer holidays (even if our own weather is the envy of those we seek to emulate), we can all throng the cities of England, America (and more recently, China and Dubai) in our shameless thousands.

We can educate and oppress our colleagues upon our return home, about Big Ben, and Shepherd's Bush. God Bless the Queen. We have seen the Statue of Liberty in New York. Never mind that basic liberties still elude our peoples.

We can even recite the obscure second verse of the American National Anthem (The star spangled banner), by heart. All our tailors (or fashion designers, as they now prefer to be called), are supposedly London trained; A required bold faced lie to assuage the ego of potential clients.

Even the enterprising Igbo man (of eastern Nigeria) now has to put "made in Italy" Labels on his otherwise creative products.

The justice system has not fared better. Many of our Judges are only comfortable after finding support for their decisions from the eighteenth century observations of a judge in England who was deciding a case based on his perception of the then realities of the English society.

Academicians who should help shape society by articulating imaginative new policies, are either embroiled in import license fights, or are being run out of town by nincompoops in government who are seeking to define limits to what can and cannot be taught in schools for goodness sake.

The way I see it, the real heroes are those being sanctioned for teaching more than they are paid to do. It only means they care, whether one agrees with their sincerely held opinions or not. If only those who carry guns of coercion can also exercise their assumed mandate with compassion and vision, then no one will have to look over his or her shoulder for enemies, real or imagined.

One could spend a life time merely pointing out shortcomings in our social institutions. No constructive purpose would be served. It is nevertheless sobering that one might have died in vain in the pointless pursuit of the symbolic golden-fleece in Canada. One would have become another faceless statistic. The cause of death lost on the people whose proud heritage one sought vainly to defend.

A question continues to plague my mind though. Should the unthinkable had happened to my colleagues and I in the heat of the racial brouhaha generated by the old man, would it have been worth the ultimate sacrifice?

If sometime in the future, we are called to risk life and limb in order to protect the dignity of the mother land, will the average citizen consider it a privilege, or an early parole to merciful death? The question continues to linger.

REVIEWING THE NIGHTMARISH REIGN OF THE MEN WHO HAD EVERYTHING
(And the endless cycle of missed opportunities)

"One of the most difficult things to cultivate is a strong will".

Post election eve, 1983. It was getting very late. Even my eye lids were heavy with bearing the brunt of lack of sleep. It had been a long day. I braced myself for the usual battle of securing even a foothold on one of the over crowded late buses going my way.

Oshodi bus stop was (and more so now) notorious for its army of pick pockets. Even most of the buses in service were major accidents waiting to happen.

While I reminded myself not to let my guards down enough for some crook to meet his quota for the night, I was too tied to begin a debate with myself on the wisdom of entrusting life and limbs to a tipsy driver of a "Molue" bus that is probably on its last few gasps. The ultimate wisdom counseled an onward match home by any means possible.

Oshodi bus stop is not a safe haven for the meek or the faint at heart. So, with understandable, but well managed trepidation, I listened patiently to the bus conductors' invitation to treat.

The crucial "Agege Straight", indicating the bus was going my way, was not forth-coming. I must have been at the bus stop for close to two hours. I could not afford the luxury of a dangerous taxi cab at such a late hour.

The prospect of being held hostage and possibly maimed by hoodlums posing as passengers in a taxi cab did not appeal to me. There was some relative safety in the noisy rowdiness of an over crowded Molue bus. The trouble was to succeed in fighting through the barricade of pick pockets unto one of such buses.

Unfortunately, in recent times even buses no longer offer the safety in numbers that they use to. Not with the spate of **"ONE CHANCE"** abductions where hoodlums kidnap and rob unsuspecting bus passengers. But I digress.

Never mind that while on board, I may be berated, or treated to the ultimate display of marketing ingenuity, (depending on your sensibilities) by unauthorized peddlers of pharmaceutical products of which a single dose is alleged to be so potent, it treats such disparate ailments as headache; stomachache; male impotence, female infertility and river blindness.

You also have shifty-eyed religious merchants, or pushy passengers insisting on extra elbow room in an already cramped space.

After what might have seemed like an eternity, I somehow found a bus going my way. I even had the luxury of a seat to myself. I flopped tiredly on my seat, oblivious to its hardness, and the stench that hung ominously in the rather humid bus. I must have dozed off instantly. Sure enough, I was eventually aroused from my slumber by an argument that had developed while I slept.

Expectedly, the ruling National party of Nigeria (precursor to the current ruling PDP) had secured a landslide verdict from Ovie-Whiskey's Federal electoral Commission (WHICH WAS ALSO THE PRECURSOR TO THE IWU LED INEC). The nation, to say the least, was very restive.

The individual at the center of the argument in the bus had been raving noisily in self congratulation on account of the electoral out-come. Majority of the passengers were on account of their political leanings naturally chagrined by the apparent electoral fraud. All felt compelled to abide by the verdict. Few were however willing to have their noses further rubbed in it.

The garrulous celebrant even volunteered that he was one of Bayo success' legendary political enforcers (alleged thugs, for short). He even arrogantly urged the miffed passengers to croon "One Nation", in unison with him. At the time, the expression, "One Nation", was the victorious political Party's slogan.

Having recognized that the NPN slogan of 'one nation' was no more than a shamelessly cynical affectation at national unity, I was not surprised that none of the passengers heeded his call. Instead, he succeeded in generating a brouhaha that veered dangerously on the periphery of actually leading to physical violence. Philosophically, I was saddened by the development. Nevertheless, I continued to watch the argument unravel with detached indifference.

I was too tired to care how it was eventually resolved. May the good guys win, I hoped, timidly. Presently, some began to take the political affront personally. The fierce exchanges and the verbal diatribes were getting more heated and rather personal.

It was bound to get out of hand. I looked anxiously to see if I was nearing my destination. I did not care to get caught in the inevitable cross fire.

The bus came to a stop. Thankfully, it had reached my stop. I disembarked gratefully. The argument was already getting ugly.

I was happy to be out of harm's way, I thought. "Now, I can get some rest and prepare for tomorrow's battle with life", I cogitated.

No thanks to the hopeless transportation system and the even more atrocious condition of our roads, people working or schooling at any significant distance from where they live only have a chance for a few hours of sleep before waking up again, well before dawn, just to beat the predictably maddening chaos and traffic congestion which could and ought to be easily solved with subterranean rail service.

I was thankful to be home anyway, even though I could barely make its shadowy silhouette out from under the spell of darkness that much of the city was cast. An even more predictable development, since incessant power failure, for us, has become a seemingly inescapable way of life. As a critical aside, will the anti-corruption agencies really investigate the Obasanjo administration's handling of all the billions allegedly spent between 1999 and 2007 on new electricity generation and delivery infrastructure?

Unfortunately, I did not reckon on the diabolical schemes of the offensive passenger who had everyone in the bus riled, except a disinterested me.

Evidently, that was my mistake. My non-aggression pact with myself had been lost in the sea of his inebriated consciousness. He had promised to visit thunder and brimstones on someone in the bus for lampooning the victorious "Naira Party of Nigeria".

Since I had not partaken in the free for all, I naturally assumed I would be immune from the hostile visitation by the gods of vengeance. Unfortunately for me, our overzealous political cheerleader had suddenly suffered a memory ambush. He came after me with a premeditated vengeance.

He held the collar of my now crumpled shirt tightly against my throat with a very huge hand, and weaved drunkenly; "Where u tink u are going?" he challenged, rather menacingly. "What?" I responded, aghast by his rather quarrelsome demeanor. His scarred face was contorted in a vicious rage, making him look eerily demonic from close range.

Of course, all the while his massive hands were straining wickedly against my throat, interfering with my circulation, and my subjective perspective, even as I now relate this ordeal.

Who would now blame me? You never really see your life flash before you until a vice grip locks around your neck.

At a stage, I worried more for his life than mine. He was so engrossed with being angry at the world (meaning me), that it was a real chore for him to go through the ordinary routine of inhaling oxygen, before blowing out his abundance of hot air.

"U tink u fit run away with your big mouth? He sneered, taking reckless liberty with the Queen's English, (and my throat, while he was at it).

The stench of his breath reeked with alcohol. He was too far gone. "Say one", he commanded, assuming a professorial air, in spite of his drunken state.

"Me?" I challenged, rather apprehensively. All the while, I was wishing the nightmarish episode to dissolve into one of those embarrassing dreams you share with only trusted friends. I was going to awake shortly into a kinder, and gentler world (a la George Bush.).

"Say one" (which was a shortened version of the then NPN slogan), he repeated with increasing impatience. No, this was not a dream. Even Pollyanna's eternally boisterous fantasy world of love and good cheer could not wish this away.

In any event, I have a guardian angel, and the rest of the story is now history. He was soon apprehended by a police officer, who, unknown to either of us, had apparently been quietly seething at his rancorous conduct in the bus. The officer was finally presented with a good excuse to put the cantankerous clown in his place.

I have always deplored police brutality. This was no exception. However, this particular show was apparently put on in defense of my rights; such as they are.

Later, the officer inquired whether I intended to press charges. Looking at the ruin that once was an arrogant loud mouth, I was suddenly overcome with compassion (for those the police officer must have manhandled in the past of course. Whom did you think I was feeling sorry for?).

"No I would not press charges", I said. The wisdom of the decision has little to do with any act of forgiveness. The futility of such an endeavor will soon become clear. To be sure, this thug was just another pitiably misinformed citizen who (in the unending battle for the soul of this nation, nay, this continent) was being used as a foot soldier in a dialectic battle he could never fathom.

In any case, I was just too tired to be bothered with oppressing the hapless pawn with the legal system. I was also not prepared for the usual police custom of asking for some mythical "particulars."

Dismissing officials (whether police or customs) at most check points with a pathetic fifty kobo (which then was the equivalence of fifty cents, at the highway check-point may be excusable. Insulting them with such a paltry sum (which I did not even have to spare at the time) at their station may be too much for them to abide.

The moral here is that during the defunct Second Civilian Republic in Nigeria (and I am sad to report that even now, during this imperiled fourth republic) the politicians had the power of life and death. They even had the privilege of hearing reluctant electorates say "one" (or its current equivalence).

You could do it voluntarily to win a government contract. You could be gently prodded by muscle flexing hoodlums to sing the political favorite tune, and to sing it with sufficient feeling.

Either way, millions of the population greeted the now maligned ruling party with the slogan, "One Nation, one destiny".

The party could not have secured its historic (FEDECO AWARDED) landslide without those coerced or contrived shows of support. The event of their victory could have been more noteworthy, had they only heeded the admonishment of their otherwise soothing slogan.

For a while there, they really had it made. However, like the prodigal sons that they are, they blew it big time.

AN ENDURING—NATIONAL INSECURITY
-the most basic obligation of any legitimate government is to protect its citizens.

Very close to the police station at Ikoyi, in Lagos (the economic nerve center of Nigeria), right on (and sometimes just before getting on) to the famous and well traveled FALOMO BRIDGE, robbers operate NOT ONLY AT NIGHT TO ENSNARE UNWARY TRAVELERS STUCK IN TRAFFIC. THEY OFTEN OPERATE IN THE OPEN GLARE OF SUNLIGHT; UNHURRIED AND UNAFRAID BACAUSE THEY KNOW HELP IS NOT ON THE WAY TO PROTECT CITIZENS WHO HAVE GROWN ACCUSTOMED TO BEING OPENLY ASSAULTED AND ROBBED. CITIZENS WHO HAVE GROWN USED TO POLICE OFFICERS AND OTHER LAW ENFORCEMENT FOLKS COLLUDING WITH ARMED BANDITS.

Now, think about it. Ikoyi is supposed to be one of the very few high brow areas in Nigeria. Yet armed bandits operate there openly and with impunity. Imagine what takes place at less "protected" areas of the country.

It is now the standard practice for most people who could afford it to hire POLICE ESCORTS for protection whenever they are venturing outside the barricaded walls of self-created prisons (they call Homes).

With the growing spate of targeted assassinations, arbitrary robbery incidents, maddening traffic congestions on poorly maintained roads coupled with daily road side extortions by police officers assigned to patrol those roads, it shouldn't surprise many that a number of the well-heeled in society rarely leave the safety of their sprawling (homes) 'garrisons.'

I again recall the poignant experience of the late Mr. Aruede. During his lifetime, he was probably one of the most hardworking people in Nigeria. He stood steadfastly on the right side of the law. He was a quiet businessman with fond hopes that his children will grow to live in a better Nigeria. He made no waves.

On this fateful day several years ago, under the blazing afternoon sun of Lagos, he made his way to his bank at Ilupeju-Estate, Lagos. He needed to make a quick withdrawal; a wary chore that use to take all day.

So much for efficient bank service in twentieth century Africa! The sum he needed was considerable. It had to be, to willingly elect to spend much of the day on an endlessly long cue that snaked grudgingly to intemperate and (at the time) probably underpaid tellers whose demeanor belied the true nature of bank transactions.

You would think many of them were the obfuscated relations of a very wealthy man who was forcing them to help give all his money away! But do their attitudes change when you are making a deposit to their imaginary uncle's coffers? No!

You almost get the feeling that they would rather you stuck with the pre-industrial practice of hiding your treasures behind the barn door or under the mattress. But I digress with overwhelming flourish. Blame that on years of pent up disgruntlement

Mr. Aruede arrived at the bank early enough. Immune to the frustrating drudgery of the cashiers, He waited his turn. After several hours of tested patience, he completed his transaction at the bank. Discreetly, he tucked the bundle away from view.

He was a careful man. He left the bank, proceeding to the parking area to make another grateful getaway from the drudgery of the calculated motions of people with a pathetic work ethic.

He was still in the immediate vicinity of the bank when someone on a motorcycle rode alongside him, and somehow relieved him of his precious bundle. Another battle seemingly lost to the army of street marauders?

The rogue was eventually apprehended. Actually, it was mostly a single handed, partly heroic, partly a desperate last stand by a hardworking man who was probably one of the most victimized honest men in the Country.

I will not distract you with the titillating tale of his one man capture operation. The truly revealing story began and unraveled itself at the Ilupeju Estate police station.

He sat there waiting for the appropriate officer to be sufficiently inspired to take his statements with a view to formalizing charges against the unsuccessful pilferer.

Mr. Aruede is a well versed and versatile intellectual. However, in spite of his learning, he still received a very instructive crash course in police operations. And he learned all these while he waited patiently at the station. He is not by any means naive. But witnessing first hand how the police handled a specific crime report was most arresting.

While Mr. Aruede was ruminating about the almost wasted day, a police officer hurried into the station in obvious distress. He had just been relieved of his gun by some audacious assailants near Palm grove bus stop in Lagos. He was obviously a rookie.

One of his superiors told him not to be dismayed. The superior officer went out and came back after a long while, with the gun. All the while, Mr. Aruede sat there waiting for justice.

Amused by this new development, he followed the proceedings. The superior officer told the rookie cop that he had helped retrieve his gun. He advised him to show proper respect to certain deserving people in the future.

Obviously speaking cryptically, he pointed out that the occasional whims of those in business rapport with the police should be duly accommodated. The Palm grove thugs had evidently paid their dues.

Naturally some questions begged for answers. How did the police officer know the particular people who took the rookie cop's gun? How did he know where to locate them? Why did the police not consider prosecution?

Mr. Aruede, a man not easily dazzled was evidently shocked. These men were obviously accommodating criminals and did not care who knew it. He concluded he had seen enough. The painful impression was that the police work hand in hand with thieves and lowlifes they were being paid to investigate. He was no longer going to press charges.

This account is merely reflective of a series of self indictments by the police force. It is therefore not surprising that in spite of the several road blocks (some call them toll gates), armed robbers still ply our roads as if they own the land. They would certainly not have been so successful had the police been determined enough to crush them.

Any doubts that the police are capable of being effective is dispelled by the remarkable success they have in apprehending cop killers, and bringing them to prompt justice.

Another documented instance of police-criminal collusion happened in one of the police stations off the Lagos-Ibadan express way.

A woman and her son, (who shall remain nameless), were attacked by armed robbers. They were both beaten and humiliated. Their car was stolen.

Eventually, they found their way to a police station in a nearby town. And to the credit of the police, within a short time thereafter, the culprits were apprehended.

Routinely, the woman was asked whether she intended to press charges. Meanwhile, a well dressed man had come to the police station requesting an audience with the battered lady. The man confirmed that the apprehended men worked for him.

He promised that the lady's car would be repaired like new and returned to her. He even presumed to immune her against all future robberies, stating that should she be inadvertently robbed by anyone, he would personally ensure that her stolen property is traced and returned safely to her.

He made all this fantastic promises subject to one condition. She must drop her allegations against his henchmen. He confided that even if she did press charges, the police were amenable enough to eventually find a way to set his boys free. He assured the confused lady that he was not unknown to the police.

He further hinted that he knew where the lady lived with her vulnerable family. The unspoken threat being, no one, least of all a hapless and uninitiated lady like her is immune from the long arm of the lawless.

So when the police again requested if the lady intended to file formal charges, her answer was predictable. She was still a young woman, determined to enjoy what life had left to offer.

She had innocent children to put through school, and an aged mother who would be devastated and helpless without her. "No", she was not going to press charges. "It had all been a terrible mistake", she stated. She was sorry to have troubled the police. She did not know what came over her.

Her bruises were caused when she was replacing her flat tire. These wrongly accused gentle-men were merely trying to be helpful. She was just being paranoid in mistaking their kindly intentions to be diabolical. She hoped they could still find it in their kindly hearts to forgive her. It would not happen again, she promised.

If the police was not aiding criminals as the convicted officer Iyamu and his ilk demonstrate they do, the educational qualifications of many in the force are a source of critical concern.

The limited learning makes many of them needlessly cantankerous and ill mannered in addressing motorists. Someone should point out that being crude and rude will not compel respect from anyone. It only betrays their limited ability to intelligently express themselves without being needlessly belligerent.

Even the reckless abandon with which some of them have used their guns and batons on defenseless civilians calls for a review of the police training program and our criminal justice system.

At least sixty percent of the members of the police force, as it is presently constituted, have no business wearing the uniform they have so shamelessly defiled. Government should let the dead weights among them go and recruit people with better education, dedication and training in crime fighting and public relations.

Their task is to protect law abiding members of the public, not to maim them. Even alleged criminals have some rights too! The intelligence and corruption fighting agencies like the ICPC and the EFCC should stop chasing the shadows of imagined political opponents of temporary occupants of political office.

They should help filter out some of the dregs in the police force, the entire armed forces, indeed, those in the corridors of power who have no business being there on account of their lack of loyalty to the country and its justice system.

Regular declaration of assets should be required and investigated to reduce the incidences of corruption in public service. This is not to lose sight of the fact that the potential investigators might be equally guilty of similar acts and omissions.

However, we cannot thereby decline to make the effort at social cleansing, even if the result might be less than perfect.

It is important therefore that potential law enforcement agents are properly investigated and given a clean bill of health, before mandating them to monitor those in high places. For that matter, the custom and excise department also has to be completely overhauled.

The recent spineless inquiries into the past of some of our political Heavy-weights were a disgrace to the concept of accountability and probity in government. They may yet be re-visited by those who have the stomach for it.

There are so many millionaires in the nations military and no one seems to be bold enough to ask some discerning questions. If the military is sensitive about its past, then it has no moral right to investigate others (much less interfere in our body politic). Not that it is doing a credible job of it anyway. For example, I am certain many Nigerians would like to know how some of them came about their wealth, and how much tax (if any), they are paying at the present time.

WE THE PEOPLE
(AS AIDERS AND THE ABETTORS READY TO BE 'SETTLED')

Like most politicians all over the world, Nigerian politicians thrive on the creation of suspicion and mistrust among otherwise tolerant electorates.

It was important for them to remind us of the somber fate that would await us should any of their opponents win our mandate.

They discreetly scurry their children to safer havens in London, England; The United States, or the Far East. The farther the better. Meanwhile, they encourage us (in the name of the cause), to stake lives and often malnourished limbs in support of their political ambitions.

They were determined to win the elections on our behalf, even if they had to do it at the expense of our fragile social amity.

Nothing would please many of them better than to dance to an electoral victory song, even if over some of our dead bodies. "That is the price for freedom", they are apt to cynically intone; all the while, silently thanking OGUN, the mythical god of Iron, (or its ethnic equivalent) for sparing their own beloved kith and kin from the carnage inspired by the mindless political imbroglio they encouraged and allowed to fester.

Their general ignorance and their warped perception of what constitutes national cohesiveness were exceeded only by their conceit, delusions of grandeur, and an abiding fastidiousness.

Unfortunately, many of our people have been deluded into believing that Allah himself had anointed some of these political turn coats to be instruments of his grand design for the nation.

It was therefore their responsibility, (they reasoned), to assist those so anointed any way they could. This facetiousness in laying claim to a heavenly mandate is, to be sure an insult on the omniscient being when you consider the caliber of the people making such arrogations. If it was not such a tragic turn for the Continent, it would have been laughable.

The unscrupulous politician can live with the penury and squalor that his self-serving policies and inaction inflict on his constituents. With deft political maneuvers, it was easy to divide the people, pitting families against each other, neighbors become bitter antagonists and would-be couples are required to put weddings on hold because of feuding distant relatives.

No one is immune from the madness. Even otherwise sane onlookers are forbidden by influential family members or employers to speak with perceived enemies. Their war becomes yours. And after years of violent feuding, you cannot still clearly fathom how it all started.

Politicians are funny that way. They adopt an approach popularized by Nietzsche (the famous polemicist). They assure the rich of protection from the impatient masses, while assuring the poor of prompt economic and social emancipation.

Self—proclaimed Christians must stand sentry to ensure that the Koran is not dipped in the Atlantic Ocean as "threatened". Unfortunately, the political metaphor was manipulated to rile an already suspicious population.

Those still standing guard at the southern front should be relieved of their post. The back door had been conveniently left ajar by some of their colleagues intent on fostering personal goals at the expense of the collective (if misconceived) purpose.

The devout and fatalistic Muslim was also encouraged by the self-preserving politician to be terrified of otherwise peaceful compatriots subscribing to what they regard as dubious Christianity.

They were required to lend moral support to the feudal conservatives and their totalitarian designs of dominating the entire country.

Islamizing the southern states of the nation was a noble cause to be diligently pursued by real believers. All devout Muslims must rally behind the Jihad. But we are beginning to see cracks in the monolithic superstructure.

The pretenders and the professed mouth-pieces of the people have cried themselves hoarse. The hate-mongers are also in retreat; and the pilferers were briefly paraded before us in disgrace.

The survivors of the purge still lurk in the shadows waiting for their "new-breed" protégés (or power broker 'godfathers') to rehabilitate them politically.

These selfish hate-mongers turned us against each other. The people should turn away from any naive political neophyte that ventures to rehabilitate any of these discredited politicians.

Statements suggesting that the country cannot survive the exclusion of certain person or persons from partisan politics are desperate verdicts by diffident defeatists who have no business pontificating on issues they hardly understand.

The average Christian or Muslim in Nigeria was ordinarily tolerant of the other. However, according to their leaders, if it would promote the sanctimonious cause of Allah to hate and persecute the other, (as defined by them) then Allah's will be done.

After all, the faceless members of the Mafia (whether it be at kaduna, Ikene, or at Onitsha, may have spent all week oppressing the population and robbing the country blind, they still chair the innumerable fund raising ceremonies to help better the common man or woman. They also donate to churches and mosques, and occasionally build others.

They did not defile themselves with unclean meat. Although many of them may be of doubtful intelligence, and their minds encrusted with out-dated feudal or royal platitudes and sentiments, they were nevertheless the self-selected leaders of their people. They were very kind to beggars. They gave alms generously and protected their wives from the treacherous gaze of lecherous men with unclean thought; Men, such as themselves.

As soon as the sun tentatively set on their inglorious empire of hate, late in 1983, we took to the streets in self congratulations as if we too were not active participants in the organized infamy.

As long as the political joke persisted (as it does now, given the 2007 electoral debacle), we were all going to be active participants. Now we are ebullient undertakers; A fitting paradox for a hesitant and lumbering little giant.

Determined to have our own fair share of the national largesse that was then being freely auctioned like the politicians' private property, we bled our children's future economic insurance with shameless gusto.

Now we all must pay for the collective sins of the past. And the children must pay with us, should they choose not to flee the borders in search of greener (American green card?) pastures.

There was corruption. The stench of the political graft stunk to high heavens. Reports of scandals filled our Newspapers, and the resultant military Coup came as no real surprise to anyone, except perhaps Shagari, the hands-off president whose alleged innocence in the face of such unprecedented graft still rankles so.

By the close of the 1983 political year, the disgraceful political culture was quickly assuming a new and grotesque dimension. The country had been so ravaged until what was left of it was no more than a gaunt skeletal form of its former self.

They had consciously or unconsciously set out to brutalize the economy and trivialize our most cherished customs. They sold the soul of the country to the highest bidders, and rubbed it in by violating the trusting innocence of some of our young women.

They were brutally successful. Their regime had come to the very edge of a political precipice

The chastened population hoped that this type of inept and arrogant leadership was surely on the verge of permanently becoming a very bad memory. As it now turns out, this was no more than a collective fantasy by a bunch of slaphappy people.

It's so easy to pontificate from the relative safety of the sidelines. Criticizing and second guessing others to no end.

I have never liked the self-indulgent sanctimony of so-called 'social critics' who never take any risks or assume some of the responsibility of making things better by rolling up their well-tailored sleeves and getting their hands a little dirty while helping to lift up society from the temporary quagmires it may from time to time find itself.

I am not impressed with people who never tire of telling us how bad things are but never put themselves on the line in any meaningful effort to accomplish even some of the changes they scream about to high heavens.

Lord knows I have written, spoken, matched, held strategy meetings, gone on international Television and Radio to argue and fight for the kinds of changes designed to usher in the rule of law, social sanity and

political sobriety not only in Nigeria but in order oppressed communities around the world.

Standing on the sidelines while cynical, corrupt or mentally ill-clad tyros continue to make a mess of things, was for me no longer acceptable, despite the obvious risks to life and limbs.

Further, I shunned the self-defeating escapism of those who like wimps concede that if you cannot beat them, it is perhaps better to join them. Not if you are not willing to sell your soul for a mere mess of porridge. Not if your real objective in getting directly involved in partisan politics is to effect meaningful changes as opposed to the self-serving quest for political office, solely for self aggrandizement.

With the philosophical battle so joined, not withstanding the messy political landscape and the absence of a consolidated and focused progressive machinery, it was nevertheless clear what kinds of individuals I would likely stand up against.

During our meeting (prior to the 2007 elections), CHIEF GANI FAWEHINMI (SAN/SAM) was understandably very wary, especially given our violent and corrupt political dispensation. However, once resolved, I decided to take a modest bite at the political establishment, noting all the while that I had no illusions about the corrupt landscape. I nevertheless felt good about our chances and continue to believe I actually had the election won, despite all the shenanigans and the corrupt coalition of INEC officials, Police and paramilitary forces employed by my political opponents and the President Obasanjo's machinery deployed specifically to Ekiti State for its continued conquest (both by hook and by crook).

LET ME AGAIN BE CLEAR. THERE ARE GOOD PEOPLE IN EACH OF THE REGISTERED POLITICAL PARTIES IN THE COUNTRY.

SIMILARLY, THERE ARE THOSE WITH LESS THAN WORTHY MOTIVES WHO BELONG TO EACH OF THESE POLITICAL PARTIES ALSO.

JOINING ONE PARTY OR THE OTHER DOES NOT AUTOMATICALLY SIGNAL AN IMPROPER MOTIVE.

WHAT YOU DO WITHIN THAT ASSOCIATION AND WHAT YOU ARE WILLING TO DO TO SECURE ELECTIVE OFFICE SPEAKS MORE ELOQUENTLY AND UNEQUIVOCALLY ABOUT YOU AND YOUR CHARACTER THAN THE MERE JOINING OF A PARTY

For me, therefore, there clearly was an articulated vision and context for my direct engagement in partisan politics, despite the odds and the messy landscape. Consider the following summary of my official declaration of candidacy for the 2007 elections;

THE FOLLOWING WAS MY DECLARATION SPEECH AS A CANDIDATE FOR OFFICE DURING THE LAST NATIONAL ELECTIONS
—AN OPPORTUNITY FOR A NEW BEGINNING

"Without acts of moral courage mighty words of moral outrage are but so many fire-flies in a mason jar. Cutting through the darkness of injustice with a flicker one moment; Dead and forgotten the next"—Governor Wilder (First African American Governor of Virginia)

Bottom line, ladies and gentlemen, **talk is cheap!**

I stand here today ready to formally set my feet on a course I have always known I must follow. This represents the fulfillment of the commitment I verbalized years ago during the launching of my first Book.

While writing THE MILITARY FRANCHISE, I committed myself to drawing attention to the challenges that confront us as a nation. I believe I have met those commitments. I committed myself to highlighting a number of the opportunities still within our reach.

Over the past several years or so, I am confident I did. Further, I committed myself to working with others in finding constructive solutions to those challenges. Over the past decade or so, I have done that both in private and public settings.

I equally made a commitment to do my part in making the most of those opportunities for the benefit of the country.

This is partly why I stand before you today asking for your support and hoping that our collective passion and commitment for positive change will serve as the critical wind beneath my political sail.

This visceral commitment and a passionate belief in Nigeria's future, partly explains why THE MILITARY FRANCHISE continues to be a powerful information resource and a PROGRESSIVE MANIFESTO for anyone truly interested in solving many of the problems facing the country.

Yes, as untidy and unsettled as Nigeria's democratic experiment is today, many of us who have made a similar commitment at one time or another, cannot in good conscience continue to sit on the sidelines, waiting for things to sort themselves out.

If I believe (as I clearly do), that I have more worthwhile things to contribute towards the enhancement of the country and its people, then the time has come for me (and others with similar passion) to wade in more directly, albeit with some understandable reservation, given the country's history of electoral chaos and political corruption.

I have therefore come to the momentous conclusion that it is no longer sufficient for me to roll my eyes in disgust from the comfort of the sidelines. Of course I don't have to participate in partisan politics for me to continue having a great and satisfying life, or be able to point out meaningful accomplishments 1 have made to the cause of democracy-and social justice, whether in Africa, or the Americas.

However, one cannot down play the frustration of publicly and privately proposing constructive suggestions to current political leaders, while those in the right positions instead vacillate, cynically obfuscate, or ineptly continue to fritter away the people's finite resources without being held to account.

Given their failure and the dire straits the country finds itself today, people like me who are able and willing to make the sacrifice, definitely have to find a way to do more. For the sake of others who are actually downtrodden by the prevailing lawlessness and held hostage by decades of greed, mismanagement and ineptitude, I know I have to do more.

For the sake of keeping hope alive for the youth who still have some faith about the superiority of goodness over evil, I have to do more. In order to redeem the sense of our nation's pre-independence pride and purpose, I have to do more. For the edification of our collective national consciousness and to invigorate the coming generation who still have the vitality and the passion to accomplish true greatness, I certainly have to do more.

I have to do more, so that my children and their own children will also have the option of partaking in an enriched African legacy that my own father, the great and now late Chief Funsho Akindele, bequeathed to me.

I need to do more because at a time when some sanity still reigned in this potentially great nation, the country invested valuable resources to accord (people like) me the privilege of moral, spiritual, and academic education. I need to do more because I feel a compelling moral obligation to do so.

I have to do more because, this after all, is the time the country most needs people like me who want to actually solve problems, rather than merely talk it to death.

At a much deeper level, we are all obliged to do more even as I am reminded of the challenge to individual and collective greatness implicit in the gauntlet thrown down about a century or so ago by **President Theodore Roosevelt** of the United States. According to him:

"It is not the critic who counts. It is not the man who points out how the strongman stumbles, or where the doer of the deed could have done it better. The credit belongs to the man in the arena, whose face is marred by dust and sweat and blood. Who spends himself in a worthy cause. Who strives valiantly. Who errs and comes up short, Again and again. Who at best knows the high achievement of triumph. Who at worst fails while daring greatly. For he knows his place shall never be. With those cold and timid souls who know neither victory nor defeat"

President Roosevelt went on to note most compellingly that:

"Far better it is to dare mighty things
To win glorious triumphs, even though checkered by failure
Than to take rank with those poor spirits
Who neither enjoy much, nor suffer much. Be wise.
They live in the gray twilight
That knows not of victory, nor defeat
Nor true sorrow, nor true love"

Our nation would be so well on its way to greatness, should it be blessed with leaders, patriots, visionaries, doers and thinkers committed to these ideals of lofty national dreams, strategic thinking and purposeful actions.

I want to lend my humble service in working with others to help this nation realize its great potential. I want to work with people who are passionately motivated by similar vision and commitment, irrespective of ethnicity, gender, religion, age, or family background.

We are a couple of smart decisions and a truly free election cycle away from greatness. Personally, I am ready to roll up my sleeves and go to work on behalf of the people. The dawn of true national unity is just at hand if we allow it. A new season of amity between our various communities is just a free and fair election season away.

The people's votes must be permitted to usher in demonstrable political sobriety, leadership accountability at all levels, social sanity even-as we strive to enhance the quality of life for all citizens. And to ensure the survival of representative democracy and social equality, **WE MUST INSIST ON THE RULE OF LAW.**

We must strive for a society where everyone, including the President, the Senator, the Governor, the Judge, the Teacher, the Police Officer, the Customs Officer, the State Security Service Agent, the Government Bureaucrat, the University Professor, the Labor Union Leader, the Editor, the Student, the Laborer, the Trader, the Doctor, the Lawyer, the Airport baggage handler, the NEPA official, the Traditional Chief, the multi-national corporation, including everybody else in between (whether citizen, resident or visiting foreigner), must, irrespective of status, be subject to the objective demands of rules of general application, while equally eligible to enjoy the unassailable protections of the law in equal measure, without fear or favor.

With the resources it has pleased God to bless this nation, it is certainly in our power to end hunger in the midst of plenty. It is within our means to give hope to the hopeless and create better paying job opportunities for our teeming population.

We have the national resources to invest in the future by offering quality and free elementary, secondary and tertiary education to every citizen who wants it. It is certainly within our power to stop the oppression of the majority by a much indulged, corrupt and cynical group of unappreciative oligarchy that has wickedly kept our people under its heels and the nation's potential for greatness, far too long in abeyance.

Elected and appointed officials are supposed to be diligent and accountable public servants, not arrogant and insufferable gluttonous masters. With the power inherent in the people's votes, we have an opportunity to effectively make the views of the people finally count. We must begin to insist on electing true nation builders.

We must begin to elevate people of real integrity if we mean to reclaim the moral fiber of our nation. The people must begin to insist on making elected leaders accountable to their needs.

The time has come to chart a bold and progressive course. We must forge a new direction for the country. If we want a fresh start and a new opportunity for a great beginning, then I call on you to support my efforts and the efforts of people who share a similar commitment to the people.

I call on you to join this cause that is bigger than me, or any of us in our individual capacity.

This is a cause to rescue the nation (and indeed, Africa) from the ghoulish grasp of a few who remain equally determined to bleed her dry of its much wasted resources. They have done so for decades while leaving much of the population behind in squalor, want and disease.

While many in government are awash in wealth and privilege, our communities lie in waste and ruin from environmental pollution and years of conscious neglect and disrepair. Yet many of these leaders wonder why there is increasing agitation for change and accountability.

For their sake and ours, we better speak up now before it is too late. We better make it loud. And we better make it clear. We better tell them in a language they can understand.

OUR PEOPLE CANNOT AND WILL NOT continue to beg for crumbs from the very people who stole our national heritage.

Our people should not have to wait for hand outs from those illegally appropriating our national resources.

If this democracy is to survive and thrive, we must demand true fiscal accountability. We must lift up every community in every region by applying the nation's resources to meet the real needs of the people, not the corrupt appetite for additional private Mansions for leaders whose lustful appetite will never be satisfied unless we put a stop to it.

Let us start by providing education and healthcare for every child. Let us enhance the quality of life for the people by creating jobs and producing food in abundance.

Let us secure our streets from the growing wave of crimes that are often borne out of a sense of desperation, hopelessness and want. Let us renew our public infrastructure system, with major works projects, including roads, water, electricity and modern communication network that will make our nation thrive and grow in the new information age.

Let us create valuable partnerships around the world that will serve mutually beneficial interests. Let us dream big and aim hire because it is worthy of us and well within our reach to accomplish.

These should be the minimum standards we set for any government or future aspiring leaders. All the officials we elect must be people willing, able and undeterred in their commitment to the accomplishment of these basic goals.

Anything less should be unacceptable. Failure or ineptitude in the name of ethnic or regional loyalty should no longer be tolerated.

Therefore, if the people support candidates all over the country who are dedicated to the lofty and hopeful goals highlighted above, it will dramatically enhance the quality of life for everyone across the country, irrespective of region, ethnic group, political party, or other social affiliations.

This singular decision by the intelligent voting public will create a national momentum. In that kind of progressive environment, it will matter little which village a particular elected official comes from because his or her commitment will be to the entire constituency, not a small section or an individual (godfather).

That is the kind of leadership our people need. That is the kind of leadership I will provide if accorded the opportunity to serve.

With your critical support, ours will become a rising tide for change. And rest assured this rising tide for change will surely lift every boat!

In order to accomplish this electoral victory for the people, the support of people like you will be critical. We must all come together, even as they seek to divide and conquer us politically. We must remember that it is about us living and thriving together.

Yes, it is true that our Tribes and tongues may differ. But like our old national anthem admonished us, in brotherhood we must stand!

Service to the people is about love and humility, not arrogance and personal greed. It is not about division. It is about uniting our people around patriotic causes and a positive vision.

It is not about what they say they will do in the future. Instead, we should ask ourselves, what positive things have they in fact done in the past when they had the opportunity and the privilege of Political Office?

At the end of the day, it is up to us. If we choose to be deceived again, we are the ones who will bear the consequences. Remember the saying; fool me once shame on you, fool me twice, shame on me.

Having been fooled and deceived in the past, don't you think the country has about had enough of the failed promises and wasted opportunities by the same old group?

It is within our power to break this cycle of hard knocks, hard luck and hard times. The upcoming 2007 (and future) elections represent the next best chance for our nation to turn things around by electing the right kinds of leaders.

Stand with me, and I will stand up for your rights. Help this electoral effort, and I will work with others to help you lead this country in the direction we can all be proud.

Lend your support and remain vigilant, and I will wake up each day thinking through and working hard on things that matter to you and your families; a focused commitment that will make you sleep better at night.

Encourage your friends to join us and together, we can truly realize this opportunity for a positive new beginning.

It is when we finally reach this promised-land that we would be able to sing the **INVICTUS** with the poet WILLIAM HENLEY (1849-1903), who reminded us why we need to buckle up and steel our backs in the following verse:

> **"Out of the night that covers me**
> **Black as the pit from pole to pole**
> **I thank whatever gods may be**
> **For my unconquerable soul**
> **In the fell clutch of circumstance**
> **I have not winced, nor cried aloud**
> **Under the bludgeoning of chance**
> **My head has been bloodied but unbowed**
> **Beyond this place of wrath and tears**
> **Looms, but the horror of the shade**
> **And yet the menace of the years Finds and shall find me unafraid**
> **It matters not how strait the gate**
> **How charged the punishments the scroll**
> **I am the master of my fate**
> **I am the captain of my soul**

Let our people reclaim their right to define their destiny through leaders that will give voice to their needs and their aspirations. Nigeria has long suffered under the condescending conceit of arrogant political task masters.

Though bloodied by the failed leadership of the past, the Nigerian spirit is yet to be broken. Right here, right now, we have a chance to help it reclaim its focus and steer it towards a new positive beginning.

I strongly urge you all to support this effort for positive change any way you can. Do it now and do it with a winning enthusiasm. And tell your friends to do the same.

Thanks for listening. Thanks for your enthusiastic reception Thanks for your anticipated support which is very much valued and will never be forgotten or taken for granted.

THE ABOVE PUBLIC SERVICE MIND-SET OUGHT TO BE THE RIGHT APPROACH AND MOTIVATION FOR ANYONE SEEKING POLITICAL OFFICE NOW OR IN THE FUTURE.

SEEKING ELECTIVE OFFICE SHOULD BE ABOUT SERVING THE PEOPLE; LIFTING UP COMMUNITIES. CREATING OPPORTUNITIES AND LEVELING THE PLAYING FIELD FOR THE UNDER-DOGS IN SOCIETY SO THEY TOO COULD LIVE OUT THEIR DREAMS.

**PUBLIC SERVICE SHOULD BE ABOUT NOTHING LESS.
FROM MY PERSPECTIVE, IT ENTAILS A WILLINGNESS TO SACRIFICE PERSONAL COMFORT AND CONVENIENCE FOR A GREATER CAUSE.**

GETTING OUTSIDE YOUR COMFORT ZONE IF YOU MUST!

The following is a few sampling of the lifestyle, status and comfort I was willing to sacrifice (and which many in similar circumstances, whether in Africa or abroad) must be willing to put in abeyance for causes greater than themselves.

Anyone who talks a good game about wanting to fight for positive change, yet unwilling to make these types of sacrifices is just whistling in the air!

PROMOTING A POST-PARTISAN GENERATION

Dr. Akindele with former Governor, Niyi Adebayo (at a recent event)

CIRCA December 2005 USA—Deputy Director, Akin O. Akindele at a Christmas party with members of his Settlement Agreement Staff. The team was put in place to implement two Court sanctioned Consent Decrees. The two court orders were in place to respectively enforce equality of access for a minority group and also for women who had suffered systemic exclusion in the hiring practices of a United States Federal Agency).

- Among those at the event are—Maple, Dennis, Kimo, Terry, Wendy, Markette, Joyce, Renee, Maxie and others in the background

Other members of my dynamic Staff—Janet, Joy, Lajuana (and Tyrone, a former staff member) present at the 2005 Christmas party

All of these (former) professional colleagues are good people who care passionately about what they do and how they could positively impact the American society by diligently and proudly performing their respective roles in the quest to ensure ultimate justice for all concerned and humble accountability by the executive branch of the mighty United States government that nevertheless recognizes that it too is **SUBJECT TO THE RULE OF LAW!**

WESTERN WORLD—THIRD WORLD—WORLD'S APART

THESE ARE SOME OF THE TYPICAL COMFORTS YOU WOULD GENERALLY TAKE FOR GRANTED AND FREELY ENJOY IN THE UNITED STATES AND OTHER WESTERN COUNTRIES WITHOUT TREPIDATION OR SELF-CONSCIOUSNESS

In Nigeria, we generally have to shield ourselves and personal assets BEHIND TALL BARRICADED FENCES. **And when you can afford it, travel around town with ON DUTY Police officers serving as your personal bodyguards! These facts given prevailing insecurity raise so many other obvious questions, but that is the point isn't it?**

'GROWN UP TOYS' ARE AN ESSENTIAL PART OF THE PURSUIT OF HAPPINESS

Alas, thanks to the uncaring and corrupt national leadership, the major waterways in Africa are now under siege by **PIRATES and other self-help groups determined to inflict THEIR OWN BRAND OF TERROR!**

It used to be that Nigerians had places of leisure. Imagine hitching a boat to your SUV and attempting to go out on the water to have fun in Lagos without being hassled by BEACH TOUTS, AREA BOYS AND BRIBE SEEKING POLICE OFFICERS!—JUST PART OF THE OBSTACLE COURSE!

Sadly, the reality is that these basic comforts are out of reach except for the very wealthy in Africa. Not surprising since cell phones were, until very recently, considered a luxury for only the rich in Nigeria.

THE PEACE AND QUIET OF LOUNGING IN AN **UNFENCED BACKYARD** IN ANY MAJOR CITY IN NIGERIA IS BECOMING MORE AND MORE OF A HIGH WIRE ACT FOR THOSE WHO OCASSIONALLY DARE TO LINGER IN AN UNFENCED AND UNGUARDED ENVIRONMENT.

NOW I DEFY MOST OF THE CURRENT LEADERS TO ATTEMPT TO DO THIS IN THEIR HOMES IN NIGERIA WITHOUT TALL FENCES AND AN ALERT SECURITY DETAIL.

When people are barely able to make ends meet, or unable to get out of the maddening traffic congestion in Lagos, they are less likely to make time for little LIFE AFFIRMING ADVENTURES OR EVEN BASIC TREATS LIKE A GOLF OUTING WITH FRIENDS. In fact, you could barely find any parks or places for leisure and the PURSUIT OF HAPPINESS in most of the countries in Africa. **BUT WE HAVE LOTS OF KILLING FIELDS!**

Dr. AKINDELE AT THE GRAND CANYON in the United States. This is one of the most amazing natural wonders of the world. Its sheer size and scope is a humbling reminder of the interconnected nature of our humanity; A recognition that there are larger forces at play much more profound than a narrowly defined view of the self and the ultimate worth of material acquisitions

RESISTANT STILL, EVEN AS THE GREENS BECKON—Sometimes you ask yourself, why would you want to give up your life's simple pleasures for the chaotic and dangerous world of African Politics? There is no logic to it. **IT HAS TO BE INSPIRED BY LOVE AND DEVOTION TO A GREATER CAUSE.**

IN THE INTERIM, AFRICA IS STILL AIMING FOR THE MIRACLE OF 'A HOLE IN ONE'—A TIMELY REDEMPTION FOR AFRICA WHERE THERE IS REAL HOPE OF A BETTER LIFE FOR THE AVERAGE CITIZEN AND WHERE TRUE GREATNESS IS POSSIBLE AGAIN!

THE ABOVE PICTURES GIVE A LITTLE WINDOW INTO SOME OF THE LIFESTYLE CONVENIENCES AND COMFORT I WAS PREPARED TO LEAVE BEHIND IN THE UNITED STATES, IN ORDER TO BACK UP DECADES OF "PROGRESSIVE MINDED RHETORICS" AND OFFER MYSELF AS A CANDIDATE IN THE HUMBLE SERVICE TO (AND POTENTIAL UPLIFTMENT OF) FRUSTRATED ARTISANS, ROAD TRANSPORT WORKERS, VILLAGERS, FARMERS, GOVERNMENT WORKERS, STUDENTS

AND OTHER RESTIVE YOUTHS IN NIGERIA WHO HAVE LONG BEEN CONSISTENTLY LET DOWN, CYNICALLY LIED TO AND UTTERLY IGNORED BY AMBITIOUS HYPOCRITES AND SELF-SERVING LOCAL WAR LORDS.

OBVIOUSLY, HAD I SECURED THE POSITION CONTESTED FOR, IT WOULD HAVE BEEN A SIGNIFICANT FINANCIAL STEP DOWN FOR ME, ESPECIALLY GIVEN THE CURRENCY EXCHANGE RATE WITH THE DOLLAR AND MY DETERMINED RESOLVE NOT TO PARTAKE IN THE ORGY OF POLITICAL GRAFT AND MASS CORRUPTION.

HOWEVER THIS WAS A SACRIFICE I WAS SINCERELY AT PEACE TO MAKE IF I COULD TRULY MAKE A POSITIVE DIFFERENCE IN THE LIVES OF OTHERS. I WOULD NOT DO IT FOR ANYTHING LESS. NOT THE TITLE OF OFFICE, OR THE ILLUSION OF STATUS.

I WAS PREPARED TO TAKE THE FINANCIAL LOSS IN EXCHANGE FOR THE EFFECTIVE AUTHORITY AND CORRESPONDING ABILITY TO MAKE MEANINGFUL PROGRESS HAPPEN.

MY GOAL WAS TO USE THE MODEST POSITION AND THE IMPLEMENTATION OF MY WELL DETAILED AND WRITTEN PROGRAMS FOR THE PEOPLE TO INDIRECTLY PUT PRESSURE ON OTHER NON-PERFORMING ELECTED OFFICIALS TO DO MORE.

MY THINKING WAS THAT PEOPLE WILL THEN BE ABLE TO SEE THAT IF I COULD DO A LOT WITH THE MODEST POSITION (SHOULD I HAVE BEEN ELECTED), PERSONS OCCUPYING OTHER POSITIONS WITH GREATER ACCESS TO FUNDS FOR PUBLIC PROJECTS WOULD PROBABLY RUN OUT OF THEIR FALSE ALIBI OF LACK OF FUNDS AND OTHER MANUFACTURED OBSTACLES AS THEY OBFUSCATE AND VACCILLATE WHILE SIMULTANEOUSLY ROBBING THE COUNTRY BLIND!

IT IS ALSO MY FERVENT BELIEF THAT YOU LOSE YOUR MORAL HIGH GROUND BY ALIGNING WITH CORRUPT GODFATHERS

WHO COULD HELP FINANCE AND POSSIBLY RIG YOU INTO
OFFICE, BECAUSE THEN YOU WOULD HAVE TRADED AWAY
YOUR INTEGRITY, YOUR ABILITY FOR INDEPENDENT ACTION
ON BEHALF OF THE PEOPLE AND THE VERY RATIONALE FOR
GETTING INVOLVED IN POLITICS IN THE FIRST PLACE!

AS CHALLENGING AND SOMETIMES LONELY AS IT MAY
SEEM, I NEVERTHELESS COMMEND THIS APPROACH TO
OTHER PROGRESSIVES LOOKING TO MAKE A DIFFERENCE
IN POLITICS, BUT WHO, LIKE ME, ARE A LITTLE LEERY OF
BEING SMEARED AND THEIR GOOD NAME AND DEEPLY HELD
VALUES TARNISHED BY THE FILTH SURROUNDING PARTISAN
POLITICS.

THE CREDIT TRULY BELONGS TO THE MAN IN THE ARENA!

SOME OF AKINDELE'S SUPPORTERS DURING THE ELECTORAL CAMPAIGN

SUPPORTERS GETTING WARMED UP AHEAD OF ANOTHER
POLITICAL RALLY

DANCING AND CREATIVE POLITICAL SONGS, LEAFLETS
DETAILING AKINDELE'S PROGRAMS, POLICY POSITIONS AND
THE CANDIDATE'S VISION WERE A STAPLE OF THE (WALL TO
WALL) TOWN TO VILLAGE CAMPAIGN.

AKINDELE PROBABLY WAGED THE MOST SOPHISTICATED
AND UPLIFTING CAMPAIGN EVER WAGED IN THE SHORT
HISTORY OF EKITI STATE. HE VISITED EVERY COMMUNITY
(including every neglected and ill-equipped medical clinic that is mostly
unfit even for animals, much less a human-being). He also ANSWERED
ALL QUESTIONS IN ORDER TO REACH, EDUCATE, EMPOWER
AND REASSURE ALL POTENTIAL VOTERS

AKINDELE ON STAGE AT A POLITICAL RALLY

AKINDELE'S SUPPORTERS OUT IN FULL FORCE

AKINDELE (DESPITE A BAD BACK AND A BAD HIP REQUIRING MULTIPLE SURGERIES, STILL SOLDIERED ON AT) ANOTHER TOWN HALL EVENT TO MEET WITH AND LISTEN TO VILLAGERS HOPING FOR REPRIEVE FROM GOVERNMENTAL NEGLECT

AKINDELE ADDRESSING ATTENDEES AT A VILLAGE FORUM

AKINDELE (IN GREEN) AT A TOWN HALL MEETING

Giving Voice To The Voiceless—A VILLAGER STANDING TO ASK AKINDELE A QUESTION DURING A CAMPAIGN STOP

AKINDELE MEETING WITH VILLAGERS DURING HIS COMMUNITY "SELF-EMPOWERMENT" CAMPAIGN

AKINDELE attends a rally to address and respond to questions from members of another community.

PATRIOTISM—NOT CURRENTLY A PART OF THE NIGERIAN MINDSET!

Sadly, you hardly hear the word PATRIOTISM used with pride in Nigeria. In fact, when many of our leaders use that word, you cannot but sneer or offer a wry smile at the ironic implications of the relevant context.

Citizens don't need to have patriotism enforced or tattooed on their chest in order to be truly patriotic. When (as you do in the United States) have a society that values the legitimate aspirations and the rights of its citizens to LIFE, LIBERTY AND THE PURSUIT OF HAPPINESS, and the society's socio-political and economic structure is designed with this in mind, the citizens will know they are truly valued. They in return, will equally value the worth of their citizenship and proclaim it with pride!

Many who grew up in Nigeria cannot but recall the site of random dead bodies on major roads in populated areas. Beyond the ease with which human life is lost and not appropriately reviewed and accounted for, is THE LARGER ISSUE OF HOW THAT SOCIETY'S LEADERSHIP HAS CAUSED ITS CITIZENS TO DISCOUNT THE VALUE OF EACH LIFE, THEREBY DULLING OUR COLLECTIVE SENSE OF OUTRAGE NOT ONLY IN SEEING PEOPLE DIE SO ROUTINELY, BUT ALSO, LIKE AUTOMATONS, WATCHING INDIFFERENTLY AS THE CORPSE LAYING PRONE ON A BUSY SIDE WALK IS LEFT THERE FOR DAYS ON END UNTIL IT SLOWLY DECOMPOSES, SWELLS UP AND BUSTS, BEFOULING THE AIR. AN APPROPRIATE METAPHOR FOR HOW OUR RAVAGED SOCIO-POLITICAL SYSTEM PROJECTS EVEN IN A BARELY CIVILIZED WORLD!

However, when you think about this, it is really not much of a surprise. A society that does not value the living is unlikely to respect the dignity of the deceased!

But you must give Nigeria this. It has leaders who know how to live well. **Have you seen them on the pages of OVATION and similar publications?**

Never mind that they are mostly using national resources for their personal aggrandizement. At least they do it with aplomb and impunity.

These Publications have since become their PUBLIC PHOTO ALBUMS for the hapless in society to purchase and to envy their leaders 'good fortune' (from a humble distance, of course).

And as they do, to also begin to smartly adjust their moral compass in line with the corrupt order imposed from above. And to openly scrape and kowtow and eat crow, while repeating the mindless refrain that 'if you cannot beat them, you had better get on with the business of joining them.' A refrain designed to indoctrinate an entire nation into political servitude.

Well, thus far at least, they are not only succeeding, they have again begun to rub it in our faces. And we were loving (envying?) them for it, even as many of our citizens continue to look for our own 'fast track' to wealth (or a fast track out of the country and the pervading sense of hopeless, especially for those not much inclined to steal or collude in a corrupt scheme). And the few honest folks trapped inside? AS FAR AS THE CORRUPT LEADERSHIP IS CONCERNED, FUCK THEM!

Ever wonder why many native born Nigerians are reluctant to associate with each other while living abroad? Or why many of them are even reluctant to "confess" to inquiring foreigners that they are in fact from Nigeria (not Ghana, Jamaica, or as it's fashionable these days, even Kenya)!

The specter of a well endowed under-achieving big-for-nothing colossus in the middle of Africa will do that to you. If that does not tip the scale, the sullied image of Nigeria as THE (419) ADVANCE FEE FRAUD CAPITAL OF THE WORLD will probably help to tip it farther still into forgettable ignominy.

PUTTING PEOPLE BEFORE POLITICS
(The following was my proposed contract with the Electorates which I heartily recommend to future progressive candidates)

MY OWN COMMITMENT IS SIMPLE. I WILL WORK WITH ANYONE COMMITED TO AN AGENDA OF A TRUE NIGERIAN RENNAISANCE.

THOSE OF US WHO ASPIRE TO LEAD OUR PEOPLE FROM OUT OF THE CURRENT BITTER BONDAGE OF HOPELESSNESS, JOBLESSSNESS AND DESPAIR MUST ALL BE PREPARED TO EMBRACE A NEW VISION OF COLLECTIVE ACTION AND ACCOUNTABILITY TO THE VOTING ELECTORATES.

OUR ELECTION MUST USHER IN A NEW SEASON OF HOPE. INDIVIDUALLY AND COLLECTIVELY, WE MUST RESOLVE TO BUILD A NEW UNITED NIGERIA. A PLACE WHERE THE RULE OF LAW IS RESPECTED.

OURS MUST BE A NATION WHERE
ELECTED LEADERS TRULY PUT THE
WELFARE OF THE PEOPLE OVER
WARFARE;
PERFORMANCE OVER PARTISANSHIP;
REFORM OVER RHETORICS;
BREAD OVER BRAVADO;
JUSTICE OVER JUJITSU;
JOBS OVER JUNKETS;
AND HOPE OVER HOPELESSNESS.

"IT'S TIME TO RETURN THE POWER OF THE VOTE TO THE VOTER. IT'S TIME TO MAKE THE POLITICAL SERVANT BE WORTHY OF HIS PAY"—AKIN. O. AKINDELE (The Military Franchise, 1993)

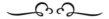

"Amidst the rush of worldly comings and goings, observe how endings become beginnings. Things flourish for a while only to return to what is and what is to be. There is perspective in recognizing this eternal cycle of life. There is a beginning for all things. And there is also and end. And the end so reached merely signals another beginning. The usefulness of what is, depends on what is not"—Wisdom of the TAO

The Military Franchise

Author: Dr. Akin O. Akindele

No. of Pages: 176

Reviewer: Segun Adediran

Many eminent scholars have written on the place of the military in politics. In the process, a wide range of literature exists to answer the ever nagging questions of why should military intervene in politics, after taking the political plunge, how should they rule, what should be the strategy and tactics of military disengagement from the political arena, how should an incessant intervention be prevented and what has been the collective experience of praetorian societies as regards military intervention and military rule. But could there ever be an end to scholars inquiries of military intervention in politics of the third world countries?

Perhaps not. That seems to be the quickest deduction considering the volume of books that already exist on the subject matter and the rapid rate at which new ones follow suit. One of such 'fresh from the print books' is titled The Military Franchise written by Dr. Akin O. Akindele, a lawyer currently based in the United States. At first contact with the book, a reader might quickly jump to the conclusion of passing Akindele's effort as one of those over-beaten debate on the right of the military to rule. Sure, it is. But beyond that, The Military Franchise can best be described as an excursion into issues and ideas that are dominating contemporary African and Nigerian socio-political discourse.

The book examines within a wide spectrum of topics the crises of development in Africa with a particular emphasis on Nigeria. Divided broadly into six sections with appropriate captions to capture each central sub-thesis, The Military Franchise begins on an explanation of the motivation that fires the writer's interest in committing his burning ideas into print. Like most authors before him who feel passionately attached to their cradles having had the opportunities of experiencing what real freedom and development are all about in other countries and what 'political domination and economic oppression' entail in the countries of their birth.

That at least was what fired up the spirit of Dr. Walter Rodney in writing the classic pan-Africanist book How Europe Underdeveloped Africa. Professor Claude Ake in Social Science as Imperialism also exhibits an hindsight of a combination of two diametrically opposed traditions in order to remove the age-long veil on western scholarship.

For Akindele and The Military Franchise, however, the issues raised are hinged on expressed inferiority complex on African race vis-a-vis its Caucasian counterpart, why the

politicians have to turn democracy on its head in Nigeria by blatant rigging of elections at each turn, how could there be so much political intolerance in the country which leaves every facet of the society fractured and what crime has Nigeria committed that after 34 years of flag and national anthem independence, visionary leadership that will bail out the nation from the throes still remains elusive. Akindele rightly captions all these 'Painful inquiries'.

However, his inquiries in the next section "Government by Military Franchise" that obviously forms the beef of the book are quite more painful than the author himself might want to acknowledge. Or what could be more painful for a people for having to contend with a constant turn-over of leaders whose only right to governance are the guns, the tanks and the raw courage to look at death in the eye? As Dr. Femi Olubanjo of the University of Ibadan once described them, these are officers, who in the main, have been promoted well beyond their mental capacity. Akindele's lamentation here is quite loud. After a run of the mill examination of all military governments Nigeria has had up to date, the author comes to (again) another painful conclusion, like other analysts would argue too, that the brief Murtala Mohammed administration of 1975/76 was the only government with a progressive direction. Others he simply dismissed as "army robbers".

With perhaps a rare-language style of a combination of poetry and prose that is richly laced with humour, Akindele elects to take position at variance with Alexander Pope, an English writer, who once argued that "for forms of government, let fools contest: Whatever is best administered, is best." At least, for him, not with what the military has administered in Nigeria. His words: "Military coups are especially uncalled for when the military itself will not introduce any imaginative improvements to the maligned superstructure." For this, Akindele draws the attention of the praetorian politicians to Mahatma Gandhi's statement that "freedom a not worth having if it does not include the freedom to make mistakes." (Pages 96-97)

But if the military will not allow the politicians the privilege to make mistakes, what is then to be done in this and other critical inquiries of the book? Akindele advances suggestions in the last section entitled "Agenda for a New Nation". No doubt, judging from his own manifesto for the nation, the author finally anchors at bay from a voyage he admits is principally propelled by love for one's nation. And that makes the book more of a product of a bleeding heart than a detached analysis of a cool-calculated head.

A well produced piece with bold print and high quality paper cover, the readers can be sure that the book harbours few nauseating errors, if there are any, that could rob the book of its well deserved place among the growing literature on "Black Man's Dilemma."

Alas, not much has changed for the better since Nigeria's independence from colonial rule in 1960.

Consider the following facts and socio-political discussions, engagements and trends summarized in this chapter. Then consider for a moment how pertinent the same issues are TODAY in the lives of Nigerians and other Africans on this so-called FORGOTTEN CONTINENT!

December 4, 2003 LETTER TO THE EDITOR

FROM: Akin O. Akindele

To: vkopytofftsfchronide.com
Cc: (Editor, San Francisco Chronicle, USA)

Subject: Your Story On Nigerian Oil Fields & The Legacy Of Missed Opportunities

Very often, the real tragedy is that as the world's sole Superpower, our (political and business leaders) miss easy opportunities to constructively engage, or reshape the world without firing a single shot, or putting young men and women in harm's way.

There is a world out there waiting to be led. Yet, positioned by destiny and circumstance, we rarely fail to take the harder road.

We allow ill-considered policies to create disgruntled new enemies, when many were poised to reward us with a grateful embrace.

I read your balanced report on Nigeria's Oil Fields with great interest. I am always glad when stories like these get reported for the world to read. I should be clear, of course, in noting that not enough light has been shed on the plight of the various oil producing communities in Nigeria.

Where many of these corporations quest for crude oil, the atrocities committed, often by Nigeria's government agents against its own people (with the complicity of, or instigation by the relevant multinational corporation), represent a new low, even for a corrupt third world democracy and its "business partners" who help to illegally line the pockets of these corrupt officials at the expense of their people.

The well documented environmental devastation and the (seemingly benign) complicity in the human rights abuses visited on the people should really shame the conscience of any civilized people.

In fact, decades of quietly tolerating successive military dictatorships oppressing the population as a quid pro quo for access to the vast crude oil reserves of the country is no less morally reprehensible than an unprovoked terrorist attack by crazed religious zealots.

The corruption and hypocrisy of all concerned professing to "care" about the people, coupled with the international legitimacy accorded the self-selected "democratic" government in Nigeria, have been especially galling and most unfortunate.

One is not too naive to forget the reality of every society or business acting with a view to fostering what it perceives to be its best interest. And from a corporate perspective, there is merit in the saying that being a good corporate citizen, especially in the community where you do business, is ultimately good for business. That alone should have inspired better and less condescending behavior from the various companies "prospecting" for more wealth from the African soil.

After all, when it comes to protecting society from wanton pollution, and the attendant health risks, the life of a child in the Delta region of Nigeria is no less worthy than the life of an equally deserving child in Middle America.

There are just some lines we never cross; not even for easy profits! If it is not right in Texas, it should not be cynically perpetrated in Abuja.

American values of freedom, representative democracy, public accountability and basic civil liberties require our political and business leaders (despite the desire for short-term efficiency and optimal production levels) to remain substantially true to the values we have sought (sometimes with good justification) to foist on the rest of the world.

The recent "confessional" by Halliburton about a history of corrupt transactions in Nigeria is clearly not unique to that entity. The SEC has rules, tame as they are, about corporate probity, even on foreign shores. Continued vacillation in the enforcement of these moral predicates ultimately endangers our very way of life.

We cannot hope to "manage" the world or succeed in exporting the values we care about if we continue to wink and nod when our "golden boys" break the very rules by which we purport to measure others.

And it matters little whether these rules are broken in the "jungles" of Africa; the restive sandy terrains of the Middle East or in secret Washington D.C. meetings co-chaired by the Vice President and Energy Industry Executives, as they purport to fashion rules designed to regulate the very energy industry!

Writing about these issues serves as a useful starting point for further actions. We must demand a more focused attention and action from those whom we have freely invested the authority to act on our behalf. Reporters asking them pointed questions in this respect, serve a powerful public purpose.

Members of the public who are adequately informed about the issues will hopefully seal the deal with their exercise of the voting power, based on actual performance father than carefully crafted photo-opportunities.

If Nigeria disintegrates, or founder from the weight of the colossal corruption and mismanagement by the current Military Oligarchy and their civilian cohorts, the humanitarian devastation will be monumental.

Your readers should know that Nigeria has about a quarter of the population of the whole of Africa. The human tragedy will be overwhelming, poignant and inexcusable. And if this turn of event develops, none of us could then deny that we did not see it coming.

It becomes more feasible, each day we tolerate our multi national corporations' illegal activities in places like Nigeria. It becomes feasible each time we confer unmerited legitimacy to a rogue or unelected government. We are avid undertakers of its eventual demise, every time we partake in the orgy of oppression and wanton disregard for the free will of its people to better manage their own resources.

Since we now have it in our power to "constructively engage" these issues, history may not forgive us if we fail to do the right thing by this friendly and potentially productive nation called Nigeria, and its so-called "nascent democracy."

Please keep the lights on, lest we further lose our way.

SOME REFLECTIONS ON THE QUEST FOR ECONOMIC AND SOCIAL EMPOWERMENT OF AFRICANS

PREPARED BY AKIN O. AKINDELE

FOR

THE UNITED AFRICAN COMMUNITY ORGANIZATION (UACO), USA March, 30, 2002 CONFERENCE

Politics and political affairs, by definition, directly bear upon how a society is governed. The political sophistication and the degree of participation by the various constituencies (interest groups) in any particular society, invariably determine whether and how the various aspirations of that group are addressed.

Let me tell you why I had to open with this comment. I received a nice message yesterday from an admired colleague and fellow democracy advocate, Dr. Ola thanking me for accepting the invitation to speak at this conference. Significantly in his message, he noted (at least twice) that I should tone down any focus on the political aspect of the topic I was to address.

Now, the Dr Ola I know is never shy of expressing his political views. So, it occurred to me that my old colleague might just be trying to ensure a smooth, positive and successful conference without making any of the invited guests uncomfortable.

Sure, it is important that I highlight the difficulty of effectively analyzing the theme of this conference while refraining from being political. However, it is even more noteworthy that your President, Dr. Ola, (speaking on behalf of the UACO) is determined to remain true to an important African creed of being a good host.

I salute all of you and thank you most sincerely for inviting me. It is indeed an honor, not only to speak at this special conference, but also because of the very salutary theme of the conference itself.

Not having been advised one way or another on this subject, I anticipate that there are other speakers and that time may be at a premium.

Therefore, I will do my best to be as brief as possible in addressing a subject I would ordinarily not mind discussing all day long.

Nevertheless, I will break my brief analysis into four (4) broad inter-connected areas of focus;

    (a) Knowledge of self (self analysis);
    (b) Preparing for a definable success;
    (e) Knowing what to do;
    (d) Securing success by overcoming obstacles

A. KNOWLEDGE OF SELF

"happiness depends upon ourselves"—Aristotle'

"Nothing can bring you peace but yourself"—Ralph Waldo Emerson

"Our actions are the springs of our happiness or misery"—Philip Skelton

Africans and African Americans are where they are today partly as a result of the vestiges of slavery, colonialism, racial segregation, military dictatorship and corrupt civilian oligarchies.

However, we remain where we are, not because of the mischief of history, or the randomness of circumstances, but largely because of some of the choices we have made, both individually and collectively (whether as a group, community or nation).

For example, we carelessly participate, or continue to permit others to use us in fanning the embers of religious intolerance, racial suspicion and ethnic bias. We sometimes tolerate, or even defend persons or practices that ought to cause us collective embarrassment. And without much reflection, we regularly pontificate about the values and benefits inherent in togetherness, without taking the most elementary steps to make that salutary vision a reality. Yet we continue to wonder why we remain marooned in managed mediocrity. Ladies and gentlemen, I respectfully submit that it not Rocket Science.

As Michael Jackson, the reputed King of Pop once said in his song,"THE MAN IN THE MIRROR"—"If you want the world to be a better place, then take a look at yourself and make the change"

Individually and collectively, we must seriously reflect on this basic challenge if we hope to effect a different outcome for members of our communities, whether in the United States or in Africa.

In fact, the word "CHANGE" segues perfectly into the next focus of my analysis. It addresses some of what we must do to prepare ourselves for the kinds of successes we crave.

B. PREPARING FOR A DEFINABLE SUCCESS

According to John F. Kennedy, "change is the law of life." Indeed, if our goal is to better our current best efforts, by striving to approximate our vision of perfection, then we should find inspiration in the words of John Henry Cardinal Newman, who said that "To live is to change and to be perfect is to change often."

Since our community (and race of people) is not even close to what we believe we can collectively accomplish or deserve, it behooves us to reflect on some of our current behaviors, attitudes and mind set, including the things we routinely do, or fail to do.

In the context of our discussion at this conference, the objective is THE SOCIOECONOMIC EMPOWERMENT OF AFRICANS AND AFRICAN AMERICANS. On paper, that objective is worthy enough. However, what does it mean really? And how best can this be attained? Now, the devil is in the details.

To be sure, I will attempt to offer my own perspective on these in the following pages. As a working principle, therefore, empowering a community is no more than making policies that will make it easier for members of that community to more easily address issues of concern to that community with new and improved tools and resources.

Since this conference is more focused on the socio-economic dimensions of this issue, I will not dwell on the political dynamics and philosophical limitations that may still need to be addressed. For additional discussions on these, I would only refer you to some of the books and articles referenced on the last page of this material.

In the interim, I will only note that, to accomplish this apparently worthy goal, we obviously must do a lot of things differently. Having not attained this goal, it follows that we have previously not done all that was necessary and sufficient to attain it. It therefore follows that, to better position ourselves for success, CHANGE is very much in order.

So, what can we do to energetically begin this process? I have a few initial suggestions;

(1) We have to build and nurture positive alliances. Our alliances must include African American brothers and sisters who believe in the attainability of this vision and perceive the direct and indirect benefit to themselves and their communities.

It must include persons of other races whose generous spirit lets them recognize that our desire to re-affirm our humanity is not designed to diminish the humanity of other races or creed.

(2) We have to jettison old strategies that will no longer wash. Blind and unsophisticated support for a person, group, or position should be a thing of the past.

In many informed circles, it is trite to note that THERE ARE NO PERMANENT FRIENDS, ONLY PERMANENT INTERESTS. We don't serve our interests and communities well by failing to keep this basic rule in mind. And without seeking to be controversial or unduly political on the subject, I should nevertheless note that, not every Democratic candidate or policy is in the best interest of our communities.

Neither is it true that every Republican policy is anathema to our interests. If we have to, we must shamelessly play the role of the beautiful Spinster and leverage whatever we have to offer, to secure some of the things we desire as a community.

(3) We have to honestly admit our own missteps and miscalculations and really take responsibility for our own current and future circumstances. Without downplaying the lingering effects of colonialism and slavery whose negative impacts are still palpable for sure. Ultimately, it is still up

to us (as a group, albeit with some help) to overcome our inconvenient circumstances.

Collectively blaming the "white man" is not only unfair, as a matter of logic, but also clearly In-efficacious. We are either going to build positive alliances, or we are going to elect to burn the bridges that would make those alliances possible. We cannot simultaneously do both. Therefore, our strategies, our actions, utterances and mind-set must be clear and consistent in this respect.

C. KNOWING WHAT TO DO

"Decisions determine destiny"—Frederick Speakman

"Decide on what you think is right and stick to it"—George Eliot

Some of the matters I just addressed also focused on identifying the things that must be done. In addition to those, the following are also instructive. According to some recent data, it was found that African Americans spend well in excess of TWO BILLION DOLLARS ANNUALLY! Yet, very little of that amount ever circulate within the African and African American communities! Some of the reasons are obvious enough.

For one thing, most of us don't take the extra trouble to actively seek out and patronize businesses owned by Africans and African Americans.

Additionally, very few businesses located in our neighborhoods are owned by Africans or African Americans. Further, there are few middle class neighborhoods in the minority communities, thereby depriving those communities of the natural socio-economic balance they need to thrive. The same is partly applicable to many African Countries who have suffered severe brain drain (and other consequential losses) as a result of massive immigration to the West.

It is no accident that in many minority communities, most of the thriving businesses are owned by people who neither live nor consider themselves a part of those communities.

Further, beyond merely paying mere lip service to the notion of community togetherness, we must now, more than ever before, let our actions speak louder and unequivocally about our commitment.

We say we admire the Jewish and Arab communities in the way they support each other's business (and leverage their power for the benefit of their native homelands). Yet, not many of us can honestly say that they have patronized a business owned by a fellow African or African American in the past twelve (12) months!

Indeed, in the African context, we certainly lack the right to be morally outraged when foreigners decline to invest in Africa when we who reside abroad are not taking the lead in either doing the same, or helping to create the right socio-political atmosphere to make this feasible.

Huge opportunities that would significantly empower us while enhancing the quality of life for both Africans and African Americans, remain untapped in many countries in Africa. Yes, we each have a duty to sell Africa's potential to the rest of the world, even those of us that have no desire to actively engage in business collaborations involving Africa.

D. SECURING SUCCESS BY OVERCOMING (REAL AND PSYCHOLOGICAL) OBSTACLES

"Opportunity is missed by most people because it is dressed in overalls, and looking like work"—Thomas Edison

"Men do not fail, they stop trying"—Elihu Root

In the final analysis, community empowerment is no more than creating a set of circumstances where the concerns of our community are given equal attention and respect by policy makers and others with whom we relate.

My thesis is therefore simple. While we need and should strive to garner support and help from all positive quarters, we ultimately have it within our reach and ability to enhance the socio-economic circumstances of Africans and African Americans.

In the Political arena where governmental entities or officials make rules and policies that impact our interests, we must organize and strategically leverage our voice, our moral and economic support and our votes to advance POLICIES that benefit us (by respectively rewarding or punishing candidates who serve or ignore our interests).

In the economic arena, we must leverage that TWO BILLION DOLLARS AND CHANGE to promote African and African American businesses and community initiatives.

In the social context, we must be engaged in the communities so as to ensure that it is vibrant with positive role models, thereby reducing incidences of crimes and juvenile delinquency. We must build bridges and pay more than lip service to our emotional attachments.

Further, we must be patient and creative in forging solutions to many of the challenges we need to overcome.

Finally, I should close by noting that high minded conferences like these, give one a sense of hope that our communities still have leaders with the appropriate vision and sense of urgency about the need to confront the multifarious challenges we face. For that, I remain hopeful and properly encouraged.

Thanks again for inviting me!

TYING UP SOME LOOSE ENDS FROM THE PAST
(Nuggets from 1999-2003—Impressions & Reflections)

BEYOND THE RHETORICS (PART 1)

Let me open with a confession. Because of the alleged circumstances of his being drafted to contest the Presidency, and the view that he did not make the most of his rare opportunity to frontally address many of the internal dysfunctional aspects of our socioeconomic and political arrangement during his last tenure, (part of the reasons why we are where we are today as a nation), **I would not have voted for President Obasanjo during the 1999 elections, if I had been in the Country, and was properly registered to vote.**

Prior to my illuminating meeting with Chief Gani Fawehinmi, I recall mentioning to Chief Falae during a private meeting I had with him in 2006 (during my pre-election outreach and consultation) how unfortunate and rather telling it was that Obasanjo avoided having a public policy debate with Chief Olu Falae, where Obasanjo's prior stewardship could have been discussed prior to the 1999 elections. But I digress.

In view of what has transpired since his inauguration, and not factoring what may yet be in the future, Obasanjo has already exceeded both my minimal expectations and my quiet HOPE that he might well surprise his many critics (me included).

Kudos to him, his advisers and the intestinal fortitude he has shown thus far as an elected President. While he is by no means the much vaunted political messiah of a bygone era, if he continues on the current path, he may well end up being one of the truly great Presidents we would ever have.

While I previously did not expect much from his administration, one should not be totally surprised that he had it in him to do the right thing. As I noted in my first book (THE MILITARY FRANCHISE published in 1993), Obasanjo has generally been an underrated leader despite his specific accomplishments (and mistakes).

I was especially proud of his activism during the various independence struggles of some African Countries in the seventies. In fact, as I noted in THE MILITARY FRANCHISE, his "DEAR MAGGIE" letter which gently chastises Thatcher, the then British Prime Minister over the South African issue, was, from my point of view, most inspired, and provided a window to the potentially progressive aspect of his soul.

Now that we have exhausted all the kudos and gotten all the mushy self-congratulations out of the way, let me focus us back on the challenges facing our potentially great nation and why we are paying all these politicians so much money and perks.

It is to help manage the affairs of our nation in a just, prudent and efficacious manner. If we believe that because we have elected them they thus must solely bear the burden to come up with all the great ideas that would move us forward, then we are not only dreaming the impossible dream, we are still dreaming it in Technicolor!

The nature of human governance makes clear that it would be impracticable and grossly inefficient to have over a hundred million people directly participate in every decision making that affects our lives, hence the wisdom behind elected representatives (whom, hopefully, we can rehire or retire at scheduled intervals).

However, as we all well know, in view of the events in our recent past, it cannot be presumed that because individuals happen to ascend to leadership it means that they have all the answers or will be sufficiently focused on matters more important to the nation.

It therefore behooves us, as the employers of these politicians, to constantly remind them of our expectations, while at the same time making useful information and ideas available to them so as to make it more likely for them to succeed.

Because, if they succeed by doing their jobs appropriately, it would mean that they have, even in a small way, done something to better the lives of many citizens.

In view of all the foregoing, I, like others, have accepted the challenge of President Obasanjo and others.

We will test their commitment and seriousness by making Information and ideas available to them and the general public for open good faith discussions, with a view to having them adopt the most prudent ideas that could be employed to advance the cause of our nation, whether it be in the area of economics, social welfare, religious or cultural amity, political reform, education or such other bread and butter or high minded issues as how to reclaim national pride and sovereignty from the various international entrapments like dubious foreign debts.

Incidentally, to respond to some of my colleagues who fret about having cynical politicians plagiarize their ideas and thereby claim all the credit, I say that, so what? If they adopt wholly or partially, any ideas that are subsequently applied to advance the lives of our people, what does it really matter where the ideas originated.

We have been beneficiaries of a great education paid for (in part) by this nation. The least we owe the country is to help it and its leaders, during its hour of need, with creative and rehabilitative ideas to ensure that the nation (and indeed the African Continent) eventually thrives.

The goal for all of us is simple enough. In our respective ways, we must help to set the feet of this nation toward the path of economic sanity, political sobriety and social stability in the interest of our children and their children's children.

Some may serve the nation through direct involvement in party politics. Some may serve by teaching and inspiring the youth and preparing them for the leadership mantle of tomorrow.

Some will serve by producing needed foodstuffs and other goods and services that will help to enhance our quality of life.

Some will help to report events, memorialize them for history and raise pertinent questions, so as to keep elected leaders honest and constantly accountable to the people.

Ultimately, we each will serve in one capacity or another. But make no mistake about it, each person's role is significant to the whole tapestry and the very sociopolitical fiber we are attempting to weave and bequeath to future generations.

It would therefore be a tragedy, if those who helped the most by putting Abacha's feet to the fire, thus moving us closer to democracy, now abandon the cause in mid stream by standing on the sidelines rather than be fully engaged in the process.

In fact, now, more than ever before is when we need their undying vision, determination and fastidiousness for justice and fair play in the governance of our nation. Some may not be well suited to govern, but they could help with developmental ideas and critical legislation.

Some may not be inclined to serve as local counselors, but they could continue to advocate for the marginalized; educate the sincere and precocious new breed politician and inspire the rest of the nation with their integrity, vision and sense of fair play.

No, the time is not apt for great minds to retire, nor is it auspicious for vibrant souls to be put to pasture. We must all function as change agents, until real and irreversible change is attained.

Therefore, having morally committed myself to this course, I intend to make the time to explore issues and other ideas on various subjects of national import, with a view to proposing specific solutions with the hope that, at the very least, it will help to enrich the political debate, thereby increasing credible options available to elected leaders who may sincerely be interested in solving particular vexing issues on which they have been given the mandate to legislate or propose policies.

Future installments will attempt to propose specific solutions to some of our identified national challenges. Enjoy the ride.

BEYOND THE RHETORICS (PART 2)—Agenda for A New Nation

To commence this national dialogue, I will start by briefly identifying three of the many important challenges and simultaneously proposing potential solutions for each of these challenges. The first is the issue of ethnicity, especially when used as a sword of exclusion. The second issue is how to ensure real quality education in public schools

The third issue that I intend to address is how the government can raise resources through taxation and the establishment of an internal borrowing mechanism which will free us from international debts and the new form of economic colonization.

Before I proceed, I must note an important caveat. Some of the ideas I will be sharing are designed to serve as supplements to other proven solutions to a number of the challenges to be discussed presently.

1. THE CHALLENGE OF ETHNICITY:

While we should continue to celebrate our ethnic heritage and use our diversity as a source of strength, we can no longer permit it to be a source of manipulation by cynical politicians and pretentious religious merchants!

Therefore, I propose that anyone living in any state should be automatically entitled to any benefits (and obligations) that citizens of that community are ordinarily entitled, including the ability to contest for and hold office, receive any government benefits, etc.

Further, without detracting from the historical heritage handed down by parents, government should henceforth desist from inquiring about the state any citizen is from (when that is intended to elicit an answer that merely identifies the "native origin" of one's father!).

In fact, anyone should be free to claim origin from the state they were either born or residing. And in any case, beyond entitlements that apply with equal force to all residents, this distinction about native origins should not be permitted to matter any more at any governmental level. Indeed, while the choice of adopted residence or "origin" is open to all, it may well be prudent, as a strategic move to dilute this challenge for the future by requiring that all newly born will be deemed to be (so far as relevant) from the state of origin of their birth (or such other states as they may thereafter reside).

While these options will by no means dissolve all ethnic challenges, they will at least limit or remove the aspect of it where government resources and power are being used to compound this difficulty.

This approach creates an incentive to make ethnicity less of a factor in our political life (while leaving it substantially undisturbed in our privately adopted cultural lives). It will also lend itself to better social amity and cultural tolerance, when no socioeconomic hay or advantages can be gained by those who would otherwise want to focus on our artificial differences.

2. ENSURING QUALITY EDUCATION:

Ordinarily, I am very wary when government tries to limit people's liberties or choices in any way. Therefore, this proposal is narrowly tailored to avoid undue burden on any citizen.

To ensure quality education in public schools, in addition to other prudent steps currently being taken by professionals competent to articulate policies and programs to attain this goal, I am of the view that without prejudice to the rights of other citizens (including civil service employees) who may desire, and can afford to send their children to private schools, any elected person (and all political appointees) should (at least for the time being), be required to send their children and wards to publicly funded schools.

Anyone that feels strongly about sending their children to private schools certainly reserves the right not to contest elections or accept political appointments.

My view is that if government officials also have their children at public schools, not only will the government be more inclined (and better motivated) to give effect to creative and effective educational policies, in fact, the needed funds will be available to hire and retain quality teachers, equipment and other needed professionals. This, if you will, is my informed self interest matrix!

3. GENERATING REVENUES INTERNALLY:

Because of the importance and fairly technical nature of the subject, I will defer discussion about the creation of a mechanism for internal borrowing by federal, state or local governments through the issuance of bonds and notes, for another date, in another installment.

For now, I would instead focus on the issue of using taxation as a key component of revenue generation by federal, state and local governments. There has to be a discussion of types of taxes (i.e. income tax, property tax, capital gains tax, and business tax), the rate of taxes, the structure and independence of the relevant tax collection agency, etc.

First, let me note that there should never be taxation without representation. This means that tax imposition (or increases) should be either directly approved by voters or indirectly through their elected representatives whom they can remove at the poles if they are displeased by their votes.

Secondly, we must have a truly independent revenue collection agency (at the federal and state levels) with powers to sanction anyone, even the President, for tax evasion, or untimely payment of taxes. There cannot be any sacred cows.

Thirdly, the issuance of tax clearance should no longer be sufficient in itself as proof of adequate payment of all required taxes. Every eligible person should be required to complete a-one page tax return information on a yearly basis with the potential of a random audit to confirm the accuracy of what was reported.

Fourthly, much of the revenues for local governments should be generated from taxes imposed, both on businesses and properties in the local government area, thus reducing any undue reliance on the "generosity or discretion" of any governor (or other official), while making funds available for appropriate community redevelopment like (some) road repairs, pipe borne water, garbage disposal, street cleaning, community bus terminals, recreational parks, paying the salaries of law enforcement sheriffs and inspectors for the community, and similar services that enhance the lives of the residents of such a community.

In anticipation of future installments to this piece, let me (by way of closing) commend you to a sentimental and hopefully motivational thought as expressed in one of my previous Books:

HOME

Beyond the trees
And all the shrubs that have turned brown
Beyond vast fields
With graying foliage and the trees' raised brow
Is a place longed for in summer or fall
Where laughter rings true
And the warmth seeps through
Where the joy is full
And every stomach too
Where families chatter
And little children matter

HOME

That happy place
Where families live and friends converge
Though dreams diverge even as we converge
Happy still is that place
That happy place
Called HOME

BEYOND THE RHETORICS . . . (Part 3)—Agenda For A New Nation

1. THE NEED TO FEED THE NATION:

No nation is perfect. Indeed, no system of government is perfect. Not even close. I have written extensively about this and its related philosophical, dialectic and economic contexts. However, that is another matter.

At this time in our world, America is by far the greatest nation on earth. America is great, partly because it is a nation able to feed itself and give some of its surpluses away as foreign aid. Beyond that, it has institutionalized important SOCIAL SAFETY NETS that have over time, proven invaluable to citizens who from time to time fall through the cracks.

Now, after decades of failed local leadership feeding many African nations on stale servings of hate, tactical tribalism, religious intolerance, and a lot of hot air sprinkled with hope, the time is long overdue for real nourishment to replenish our wary spirit and to sustain troubled souls.

According to an African Proverb, when the ability to be nourished with good food is no longer a lingering challenge, then the most significant threat of poverty or destitution is at an end; and man's basis for real worry is momentarily put in abeyance (TI ONJE BA KURO NINU ISE, ISE BUSHE).

A society that cannot produce, preserve and make available enough food to feed its people can never lay claim to greatness. This nation is currently unable to feed its citizens. Yet, Nigeria, unlike many other countries, is blessed with abundance of arable land, great weather, and a teeming and hard working population, hungering for nourishment.

Any productive society will salivate over the prospect of having over 100million people as a ready market for any product; especially food products that are a necessary part of human existence.

Therefore, any COOPERATIVE investments in agriculture by the private sector (motivated by a supportive government with prudent policies and incentives in place) will lead to a farming boom, the likes we have never seen in this country.

Now, I am not talking about the tame sloganeering of a couple of decades ago called **operation feed the nation**, which mostly helped a few fat cats to corner some choice lands for themselves and cohorts.

I am not talking about merely exhorting most citizens to attempt to do what they cannot basically do well.

Rather, I am talking about government providing real incentives for cooperative farming where small farmers can really team up to more effectively raise resources, manpower and other equipment to mass produce different food stuffs, thus taking advantage of the economy of scale.

This has to be a function of a well coordinated and integrated cooperative strategy involving both the private sector and the government.

I am talking about government providing loan guarantees and easy access to equipment, training and support for eligible persons or cooperatives willing to commit to a really large scale farming FOR HOME CONSUMPTION!

I am talking about upgrading local and other village infrastructures like roads (and other communication systems), schools, other related and unrelated businesses and recreational facilities to ensure that the quality of life is reasonably comparable to urban areas.

The goals are multiple. It is partly to provide reasons for most youth in the rural (suburban) areas to feel comfortable enough to stay and explore farming as a very lucrative and respected profession.

Government should for example provide real incentives to food processing businesses to locate in otherwise rural communities (thus making able bodied persons looking for jobs move to those areas), thus keeping much of those communities viable, including incentives for doctors and health care professionals electing to service those communities.

I am talking about giving huge (and long term) tax breaks, discounted land purchases and other subsidies to farmers and other food processing (or food preservation) businesses, including easy access to modernized equipment and facilities to produce and store food products on a large scale, including the occasional (and product specific targeted) guarantee of purchase by the government at a set fair market price (for later resale) in case farmers over produce (from time to time), or are unable to quickly move their products through the usual private channels within the country.

The goal should always be that most food items would be available to consumers for purchase even when the products are no longer in season. It helps farmers produce in bulk without the current fear of depreciation, decay or waste due to lack of adequate preservation and storage facilities.

Indeed, until private industry takes the initiative of building and renting out preservation facilities to farmers interested in this service, government may also explore temporarily getting into this venture for a fee, thus providing a needed supplemental service. This preservation facilities could also be used by government to store some extra food on an ongoing basis in case of unanticipated emergencies, drought, or for other strategic national objectives.

Clearly, the government must resist any attempts by any country to dump its own farm products in our market. This would create an unfair competition to the detriment of our local farmers.

Indeed, government may also want to institute a POLICY WHERE IT GIVES TAX AND OTHER INCENTIVES TO THOSE WHO SELL LAND TO INDIVIDUALS AND BUSINESSES PLANNING TO USE THE LAND FOR FOOD RELATED PRODUCTION, PRESERVATION OR PROCESSING.

Also, preference should be accorded foreign businesses interested in establishing facilities in Nigeria as opposed to those merely interested in exporting to the country.

This posture will not only increase direct accountability, accessibility and productivity, it will also increase opportunities for our citizens to get gainful employment and experience in the food industry.

Mr. President (and others), we have over 100million mouths to feed. The country is better served in the long run, if we empower and equip our own citizens with the means of attaining large scale food production, rather than to continue to import the food products to be consumed by retail.

God forbid we should fall out of favor with those from whom we import and they decide to punish us. We must learn from the lessons of history, and remember the good old days, before the crude oil explosion when we finally lost our innocence and arguably our way as a nation, in the wake of crazed men in power, stricken with delusions of grandeur.

I REMEMBER

Yes, I remember the guttural belching
of contented little old ladies.
The days of snow-white rice and turkey legs
and the hunger inspiring chorus line, as our women—
folk enhance the yam in tune, with the mortar and pestle.
Though the lights may fade
and the horizon seem distant,
yet, I remember my duty to remember.
And to happily remember, remains my duty still

HAVING GIVEN THESE UNDESERVING POLITICIANS A LONG ROPE TO HANG THEMSELVES, I DO BELIEVE THAT;

ENOUGH IS ENOUGH!
—THE TIME FOR POSITIVE CHANGE IS NOW

The specter of so many citizens living in squalor and abject poverty in the midst of plenty is unacceptable. Presently, few political crooks live in lavish opulence, while millions are barely able to bustle a decent meal a day. This obscene reality should no longer be tolerated.

It should shock the conscience of our world, and shame everyone that is able to help effect change. Everyone able should at least stand up now and be counted. DEMOCRACY, FOR GOODNESS SAKE, IS NOT AN END IN IT SELF. IT IS NOTHING MORE THAN OUR ADOPTED MEANS OF ACCOMPLISHING SOME SALUTARY COLLECTIVE ENDS.

Beyond the illusion of "freedom" we are fed through the media, life is not significantly better now than it was during the universally deplored Abacha years. That is unacceptable. Not after all the lost lives and livelihoods; the broken bones; the sleepless nights in foreboding dungeons; the tactical self-imposed exiles in far away lands and the daily humiliations that come with that; the lost opportunities, the unfulfilled dreams and other deprivations.

Instead of having the people's needs met, the current politicians (most of who did not believe in, or supported our pro-democracy efforts), are more focused on the same old perfidy that led to the collapse of prior regimes. They openly steal, even at the national assembly, and get away with it.

They incite religious riots for tactical political gains. They encourage ethnic rivalries and permit old grudges to fester. They foist un-elected sectional henchmen and tribal political hacks on us, merely to lay claim to some unmerited mandate.

It breaks my heart to watch the media who stood tall against Abacha and Babangida, get reduced to reporting inane rumors about some so-called intrigues among members of AREWA CONSULTATIVE COUNCIL; AFENIFERE, OHANEZE, and other potentially divisive groups when they should be focused on highlighting issues that bring the entire nation closer together.

Any one that will support an incompetent candidate merely because he or she is from the same ethnic group deserves the poor performance and neglect they receive as soon as that incompetent person gets elected.

Of course, every ethnic group is capable of producing INDIVIDUALS willing and competent enough to positively contribute at all levels of national governance.

AND SPEAKING FOR PEOPLE WHO SHARE MY VISION FOR THIS
POTENTIALLY GREAT NATION, WE SHOULD RATHER HAVE
THE COUNTRY GOVERNED BY THE MOST COMPETENT AND
INSPIRED INDIVIDUALS WHETHER OR NOT MORE OF THEM
COME FROM THE SAME ETHNIC GROUP.

AND WE SHOULD BE PROUD TO OPENLY SUPPORT SUCH
CANDIDATES. IT IS NOT IN OUR INTEREST TO CONTINUE TO
ALLOW OURSELVES TO BE MANIPULATED WITH ETHNIC AND
RELIGIOUS BIAS BY CYNICS WHO ARE ONLY INTERESTED IN
PROMOTING NARROWER INTERESTS.

To be sure, there are some current office holders who truly care for the
welfare of the people.

Those great souls deserve to be publicly identified by a responsible and
independent media.

Their tireless efforts should be supported and praised as a clear example for
others to emulate.

**Our society MUST be governed by the rule of law. Watching
Babangida, Abdulsalam and Buhari BEING ALLOWED TO CODUCT
THEMSELVES AS IF THEY WERE ABOVE THE LAW DURING
THE OPUTA PANEL HEARINGS (AND OTHER SITUATIONS),
IS AN EMBARRASSMENT TO OUR SENSE OF NATIONAL
SOVEREINGTY.**

In fact, the publicly acknowledged reality that some previous and current office
holders stole (and continue to steal) public funds without being sanctioned
is an OUTRAGE that could never be permanently swept under the carpet.

How do you motivate the younger generation to high-minded ideals of
service and general accountability when they know for a fact that some
former and current office holders still walk free living in obscene opulence
with money they stole from public coffers. GET REAL!

No amount of new laws and new corruption fighting institutions will make
a significant difference, until the existing laws are respected and applied with
equal force to everyone.

If the current leadership has nothing to hide, why should it be resistant to allowing the tools of the state from being employed to pursue allegations of corruption and other misdeeds to their logical conclusion?

Everybody is going to die eventually. And no one, not even Abacha is able to take a dime of stolen money to the after-life.

Even the favorite hiding places like the Swiss Banks and the fake backyard water tanks stuffed with cash are now no longer beyond the creative reach of a determined anti-corruption agency.

So now I wonder. What kind of legacy does the average politician invested with an opportunity of a lifetime going to show for that precious mandate when all is said and done?

More bulletproof cars to fill a parking lot? More houses in far away lands than can be slept in or used in the course of several years?

More women to entice and ravish than you can remember their names? More clothes than you can use, even if you wear a brand new one every day? Or rather, to take a different approach that long after you are gone, many will remember you and smile with gratitude in appreciation of how you positively touched their lives?

FOOLS WHO DISREGARDED THE WELFARE OF THE PEOPLE, YET PROCEEDED TO NAME PUBLIC MONUMENTS AFTER THEMSELVES SHOULD BE ASSURED THAT SOONER OR LATER, THOSE MONUMENTS WILL BE BETTER RENAMED (TO HONOR TRUE HEROES LIKE KEN SARO WIWA, TAI SOLARIN AND AMINU KANO, TO NAME A FEW), AND WHAT WILL BE LEFT OF THEM WILL BE THE BILE OF DISGUST WE WILL SPIT OUT ON THE RARE OCASSIONS SOWER MEMORIES OF THEIR TIME CROSS OUR MIND.

It is a reflection of the low intellectual capacity of some of the fools who have stumbled upon political office in Nigeria when one of their ilk is said to enjoy the reputation of "the evil genius." In our quest for a little "chop-chop", we have kowtowed too much to some of these lightweights that they have grown too arrogant for their own good. BUT IT IS NEVER TOO LATE TO BEGIN CUTTING THEM DOWN TO SIZE!

They get their inane satisfaction by depriving us of basic amenities while (in their incurable colonial mentality) it continues to make them feel important that only they can afford to travel abroad to enjoy those basic things.

When you consider that the things they try to use to oppress us are really mundane things in other civilized parts of the world, it makes you wonder what kind of infectious Bug bit these fools. Uncured and unrepentant, they are mentally trapped in this state of medieval wilderness. And there does not appear to be any reprieve in site.

If you recall, it was just a few years ago, when one of their ilk stated publicly that telephone is not meant for the poor! Imagine that level of ignorance at the very corridors of power! School children routinely have cell phones in the United States. Yet this nincompoop was able to rise under the flawed and corrupt system to one of the highest positions in our federal government!

The fact that the political entity called Nigeria was established about two hundred years after the United States does not mean that its level of development must be two hundred plus years behind.

No wonder SOME in the West look down on us and speak with barely concealed condescension, all because we continue to allow these types of people to lead us astray. Those who have traveled abroad will be familiar with this. It is amazing how we fall over ourselves to fete and elevate visiting foreigners (westerners, easterners, Arabs, don't much matter). With the connivance of this crop of leadership, we have been conditioned to accept this state of collective diffidence. **We even call them expatriates! Imagine that.**

Not very many highly skilled people will volunteer to come and live in what many consider a god-forsaken continent. COLD TRUTH, ISN'T IT?

The mostly average crop of foreigners making the move to Nigeria generally finds a welcoming society that is still stricken by the terrible afflictions of racial inferiority.

So they stay on and live large. Yet, better qualified citizens are not accorded much respect (either here at home or) abroad (where they are not celebrated as EXPATRIATES, BUT RATHER AS BARELY TOLERATED ALIENS! Worse still, equally qualified Nigerians are

not afforded nearly the same opportunity in Nigeria, as these SHORT-SIGHTED LEADERS accord lesser qualified foreigners!

The more obvious (though less significant) is the position of TECHNICAL ADVISER FOR OUR NATIONAL SOCCER TEAM.

IF THE LEADERSHIP FAILS TO SEE THE IMPORT OF THIS NEGATIVE SUBLIMINAL MESSAGE TO THE COUNTRY, PARTICULARLY THE YOUNGER GENERATION, IT DOES NOT DESERVE ITS POSITION.

And, by the way, this strange disparity in treatment starts right at our national airport.

THIS COLONIAL MENTALITY IS ONE OF THE NEGATIVE CONSEQUENCES OF THE TYPE OF LEADERSHIP WE HAVE HAD. IT IS TIME TO FIRMLY SEVER THIS INHIBITING PATERNALISTIC UMBILICAL CORD AND TO GROW UP, LEST IT CHOKES THE VERY LIFE OUT OF OUR FRAGILE NATION.

Personally, I find the sight of a Nigerian President being used as a prop or "show horse" at a so-called G8 meeting a little humiliating for a sovereign nation. You can be good friends and form strategic alliances with more powerful nations without needing to swallow your balls!

To close, it continues to be an outrage for a community to be the source of the (ill-planned oil-dependent) economic wealth of the nation, yet be so neglected and its environment so abused.

Unfortunately, having been "SETTLED", many elected politicians have lost their moral leverage to do anything about it. However, it is clearly criminal for any foreign corporation to conduct either it-self or treat our environment with less respect and consideration than it would ordinarily do in a Western society.

German multi-national, Siemens, like Halliburton, the oil company previously headed by Vice President Cheney of the USA, recently confessed to bribing some Nigerian officials millions of dollars. I am confident that this practice is not unique to this particular multi-national corporation.

While the nation must strategically open up its economy, Companies that refuse to be good corporate citizens should no longer be permitted to benefit from the great financial windfall that doing business in Nigeria potentially represents.

The old paradigm must be urgently revisited. Otherwise, the entire country may forever be lost to these modern pirates and their figure-head collaborators who have no real love for their own country.

(AFTER MULTIPLE FAILED ATTEMPTS TO FINALLY INSTALL TRUE REPRESENTATIVE DEMOCRACY AND THE RULE OF LAW, EVEN AS RECENTLY AS THE BOTCHED 2007 NATIONAL ELECTIONS—BETTER REFERRED TO AS THE HIGH NOON ROBBERY WHICH THE 'UN'-INDEPENDENT NATIONAL ELECTORAL COMMISSION CYCINALLY CALLED FREE AND FAIR ELECTIONS) We now awake slowly from the stupor. It is going to be a long wait ☹

THE FOLLOWING ISSUES SHOULD BE KEPT IN MIND AS MOTIVATION AND SALUTARY GOALS THAT MUST BE ACCOMPLISHED BEFORE WE COULD CLAIM VICTORY OVER THE CONTINENT'S AGENTS OF BACKWARDNESS AND STAGNATION:

(a) THE RIGHTS OF THE CITIZEN

Justice demands that every person be considered as having a right to equal concern and respect when political decisions affecting either their civil or economic interests are being made.

This is why we have elected representatives. There is not much divergence on this point among most credible modern philosophies.

A right to equal concern and respect, in effect amounts to treating people not equally, but as equals. Those who have less will get more access to opportunities in an effort to equalize background inequalities.

And for real justice and equality of treatment, therefore, the usual disparities in individual assets (abilities) and the unequal access to social opportunities, individuals in society would require much more than civil liberties to properly regulate their activities in a truly just manner.

For example, if there is a requirement that applicants to civil service positions must also sit for appropriate skills tests, it would not only enhance the likelihood of employing very competent people, it certainly would increase the chances of very bright people who have no godfathers at the helm of affairs in securing positions they would automatically have been precluded from getting merely because of their modest economic pedigree.

This concern for equalization of opportunities is especially germane since ours is a society where individuals tend to compare their station with others, and they are liable to be dismayed, dissatisfied or indignant when such comparisons are too often unfavorable.

Consequently, as Charles Frankel noted in his article entitled "Justice, Utilitarianism and Rights" (1974, 3 soc. theory & prac., at page 33), it is unrealistic for anyone (even Ronald Dworkin who tried in his book entitled "A Matter of Principle") to believe that once people are secure in the Bill of Rights, they would be free from plaguing envy and self doubt when they note the wide disparities in economic opportunities available to citizens that are supposed to be equal.

A society must therefore also recognize the challenges created by accidental or artificial attributes which may magnify inequalities. Certainly, hardworking and capable people with the deck fortuitously stacked against them due to no fault of theirs surely must not be ignored merely as hard luck cases.

Also, as I had previously argued, certain ascribed social positions like royalty are not only retrogressive and inconsistent with the notion that every citizen is born equal; given more recent sociopolitical betrayals of the people, it is no more than an unwarranted and often costly fascination with a now defunct way of life.

Additionally, if the guaranteed civil liberties are to amount to anything, then the same notions of democracy must extend in some limited way, to the economic interactions among citizens.

Otherwise, the civil liberties so protected under the political system, especially for the poor, will be very vulnerable, and the only really useful contents of such liberties would be those aspects that protect individuals who are well-off not to be interfered with in the enjoyment of their property; even if done in an oppressive manner.

One way to attain some form of economic equalization include the right given to employees (who are generally less well-off than their employers) to organize and form a trade union so as to be able to bargain better with rich and powerful employers.

Another example is the setting of minimum wage rate so as to ensure that those who work, at least earn enough to meet basic needs; a living wage, if you will.

The underlying implication of the views espoused here, even within a liberal-capitalist society that we appear to be striving to establish, amounts to a resolve to ensure a greater degree of equality of access to the good things of life, rather than disingenuously adopting and imbibing the traditional liberal exaltation of the narrow concerns of particular affluent individuals.

This view is a recognition of the fact that the fundamental good and cohesiveness of the group (or nation), which is the ultimate object of social justice and social formations, cannot be realized by an uncompromising and totally unregulated capital exploitation by the so called "autonomous individual".

In this regard, reference is made to the comments of Harold Laski in his book, "The Grammar of Politics", at pages ninety four and ninety five (94 & 95) where he noted that;

"Our rights are not independent of society. We have them because we are members of the state . . . . Our rights are . . . not independent of the society but inherent in it. We have them, that is to say, for its own protection as well as for our own. To provide for me the conditions which enable me to be my best self. To protect me against attack from others is to imply that I myself will desist from attacking others. To give me benefit of education is to imply that I will use the advantage

education confers as to add to the common stock. I do not exist solely for the state. But neither does the state exist solely for me" (or solely for the enhancement of any particular person, region or ethnic group, at the expense of the rest!).

After all, as Laski further noted:

"My claim comes from the fact that I share with others in the pursuit of a common end. My rights are powers conferred so that I may with others strive for the attainment of that common end. My personality so to speak, bounds and limits the law of the state. But that boundary and that limitation are imposed upon the condition that in seeking to be the best self of which I am capable, I seek in virtue of that common end I share with others, their well-being in my own. I have therefore no right to do as I like. My rights are built always upon the relation my function has to the well-being of society: and the claims I make must clearly enough be claims that are necessary to the proper performance of my function. My demands upon society in this view are demands which ought to receive recognition because a recognizable public interest is involved in their recognition."

It must therefore be noted that our struggle in Africa should no longer be erroneously cast in the narrow form of a quest for democratic civil liberties, but also for some form of economic democracy, without materially stunting the drive and fair reward for initiative and enterprise.

One must also note, by way of summary, that a theory of the unbounded self being proposed by certain libertarians cannot be stretched too far, except the suicidal object is to return to Hobbesian pre—civilization, where the self-centered life of everyone is potentially brutish, nasty and short (very much like we have in some parts of Africa, the former Yugoslavia and even in some parts of the United States where some form of anarchy still reign, either in the form of perennial drug wars, brutal political and economic exclusion of minorities or uncurbed police brutality).

This libertarian view must therefore be tempered with an appreciation of the facts of social life. The views expressed here are however not designed to suggest a reckless exploitation of individual members of society as mere means to some collective ends (however defined) as some unrestrained utilitarian would prefer. To be sure, this utilitarian perspective is no less objectionable than the theory of the unbounded self.

A more realistic account of the social contract theory should be adopted (as the basis of a new people oriented constitution). The assumptions made by John Locke about the absoluteness of certain rights must therefore be rejected.

Additionally, his argument for limited government, a view preferred and embraced by those who are well to do, and thus, conveniently "conservative" in the United States and Western Europe is unrealistic, especially for growing democracies like ours where our people need a pro-active government to help jumpstart a more dynamic socio-economic milieu.

Indeed, even the United States (did **under Bill Clinton**, and potentially **MORESO UNDER OBAMA)** IS (MORE THAN) flirting with the idea of massive government involvement at the policy level, in working with the business sector to produce policies that would both protect the local industries, and thus save (OR CREATE) jobs, while helping them to compete favorably and win in the world market as the Japanese (and more recently the Chinese) government has been doing for decades.

It can therefore be persuasively contended that, in fact, considerations of collective interests, whether under the liberal capitalist system, or any other variations of it, should, where it matters the most, override particular narrow individual interests.

It is against the background of this normative prescription that current social challenges should be analyzed, and coherent policy formulations fashioned and implemented.

The following sections of this chapter, in addition to other recommendations proffered in prior sections of this book, will therefore focus specifically on some practical suggestions that, if applied with a well articulated policy objective in mind, should dramatically set us on our way to really attaining our immense potential, economically, socially and politically.

(b) . . . Some ADDITIONAL **Practical Solutions, Stupid!**

Some may argue with merit that ultimately, the problem afflicting much of Africa is in the dearth of inspired leadership available to take real charge of our affairs. Further to the arguments that I have earlier proffered, they may well be right.

A converse view is that there are eminently capable persons out there, but they may either not be applying themselves, or need to have a set of circumstances that would focus the entire nation on what inevitably must be done, if we are to come out from under this sea of inaction and inefficacy, and dock on the dry ground of realism and dynamism.

Yes, we would need the visionary bold leaders to take us to the Promised Land. But while we wait, we lose nothing by apprising the present helmsmen of what should inform their deliberations, if they are sincere in their efforts to leave a real positive and lasting legacy for coming generations.

It is true that we want our leaders to move us from spasms of xenophobic apoplexy to a much awaited state of collective relief and fulfillment. To be sure; a leader cannot move a society to a plane of idealism if it is not ready to attain it.

However, it behooves true leaders to help society realize its immense potential for hard work, creativity, innovation, tolerance, cooperation and a sense of community.

Leadership is much more than an efficient resource husbandry. It has to be inspired and focused. It must also inspire the followers. It must always be earned by example to retain its legitimacy and credibility.

Leadership is certainly not the dominion of the few over the many. It is an ephemeral trust relationship that should never be entrenched, but terminable at the will of the people who ultimately are the real repositories of true power.

A new leader should be guided by what I have fondly named the seven giant steps of dynamism. These, briefly stated in the most general terms consist of the following policy considerations:

(1) The immediate institution or reconstitution of an independent body to oversee the collection of internal revenues, both at the state and federal levels. Government must make the filing of tax returns by all

persons (including corporations), with this thoroughly independent body, an annual event. The issuance of a tax clearance certificate, a process that is much abused, should no longer suffice as a conclusive proof that a required tax has been paid.

(2) It must also decentralize the corporate registry and the registration process, and require all businesses, whether incorporated or not to be given a tax identification number.

(3) It must speed up the radical computerization of every immediately significant aspect of the federal and state bureaucracy, and require most public employees to wear full and conspicuously displayed name tags to enhance efficiency, courtesy and responsiveness.

(4) It must send two draft legislations to the legislature providing mechanism and protection for whistle-blowers, while the other legislation makes it mandatory that certain types of decisions under the jurisdiction of certain bodies or other administrative agencies be subject to a new open meetings law so as to ensure open and good faith deliberations by public officials, and an enhanced participation level by members of the public impacted by those decisions.

Additionally, government should divest itself of any financial interest in any (internal) news organization (as opposed to having an entity dedicated to promoting the image and the interests of the country in international arenas like THE VOICE OF AMERICA (VOA) AND THE BRITISH BROADCATING CORPORATION (BBC), but should institute regulations that reflect the expectation of the public for uncensored but responsible journalism.

(5) It must setup a process of giving every citizen (and all lawful resident aliens) a Social Contract Number (and an Alien identification Number for resident aliens). This is critical for effective and efficient national planning.

(6) It must require all local governments (or states) to provide a mechanism for the registration of all title deeds to real properties with a view to planning their budgets and expected receipts, as information on the properties in their area of jurisdiction will help in projecting the number of people in the area that would need certain amount of services like water, electricity, road maintenance and other routine governmental services.

It is legitimate therefore for there to be a property tax mechanism (or a revised 'tenement rate' valuation and collection process to include a citizens appeal process for reevaluation etc), with the bulk of such receipts going to the particular local government for its annual budget and other social programs.

However, the process that would determine and regulate the taxing of citizens, whether individually, or taxes imposed on properties, should never be one that operates at the discretion of officials or government Agencies.

There must never be taxation without representation. This means, most tax increases, other than those incorporated into the constitution or other enabling legislation, may not become operative without first being voted on either directly by the electorates, or by their elected representatives.

(7) Finally, it must propose free enterprise at all levels of economic and social interaction and create an elaborate mechanism for municipalities and states to operate in certain respects as businesses for better productivity and management efficiency, while broadening their ability to independently raise money for important development projects (which itself would create more jobs) through the selling of tax exempt government bonds and other forms of obligations or securities at competitive interest rates.

This singular proposal would expand the current services (and hence more jobs) available to certain professions like accountants, lawyers, insurance companies, architects, engineers contractors and banks, to mention just a few, yet speeding up the process of the modernization and maintenance of all public infrastructures that would enhance the quality of life of the average citizen. The foregoing must however be pursued to the extent that it is without prejudice to other governmentally regulated programs like:

(a) Universal Healthcare plan for all citizens, paid for partly from a portion of the wages of all working people, municipal borrowings, and partly from contributions by both the government and the private sector with citizens free to choose from the list of all qualified doctors who would be automatically paid based on the particular services rendered to every and all patients; and

(b) **Free quality education for all citizens up to the high school (or vocational school) level at public institutions of learning. This would however be optional, as people other than elected public officials (at least for the foresee-able future) should be free to send their children and dependents to fee paying private schools.**

Having briefly laid out these rather broad policy objectives, the real meat will require delicate and thoughtful planning and deliberation with specialists in each field before reducing them into rules and administrative procedures and regulations that would then be given effect to by all government agencies as each applies to them.

In addition to the general policy statement outlined above, there are other very important issues that merit brief comment at this time as they may, if ignored, undermine the most salutary policy idea because they have to be reconciled with those policy objectives.

For example, one of the ways we could begin to defeat the negative effects of ethnicity, and truly reflect the unifying nature of our federation, is to provide that everyone is a citizen of the state of their birth.

This could be made mandatory for future births, but optional for those already born. The object of this would be to diffuse the rigors of ethnic cleavages and promote inter-ethnic unity. Additionally, any citizen who has resided in a state for a year or more should be entitled to all the privileges accorded citizens or residents of that state.

I am reminded of the saying that goes as follows; "the more you know, the farther you go". It cannot be overstated that the future of any nation is dependent on the abilities and health of its youth. Educational dynamism cannot be emphasized enough.

As I have previously argued we may want to begin to teach subjects (other than foreign languages) in the relevant native dialects so as to fully reveal full nuances of what is being taught to students who are still learning English, rather than attempt to teach them a subject like mathematics in a language they still cannot grasp, thus denying them the knowledge of the math, as well as confuse them further with force-fed English.

Our esteemed educators have always been very innovative, so I am sure other brilliant devices are already in the works. It would however be desirable if they are encouraged to bring forth those ideas and test them for efficacy. We have no more time to waste. We cannot sell ourselves short by measuring ourselves with other underachieving nations.

We have to seek to compete with the very best education systems around the world if we are to have any hope that the future generation would be able to effectively compete with Japan, Germany and the United States.

Another important area of consideration is political and electoral reform. We should make all political contributors, for example **(and the following suggested figures are purely hypothetical)**, of amounts in excess of say one hundred thousand naira to fill out full disclosure forms that would be available to public inspection, and to declare the same while applying for government contracts.

The idea is to put a public spotlight on otherwise subterranean activities of purchasing the conscience of our public officials.

Also, to really curb money politics, there should be a limit on the contributions a single individual or corporation can make to any particular candidate, say to two hundred and fifty thousand naira (to a single candidate or a ticket).

Indeed, there should also be a limit of (say) one million naira that a candidate could contribute to his own candidacy, and in case of a joint ticket, two million naira for both, and the junior party on the ticket cannot contribute more than fifty percent of the total limit. Also, all political contributions should be excluded from forming part of the tax deductible expenses.

Additionally, all candidates for office must declare all assets in their names or in which they have beneficial interests. All elected officials must annually declare their assets and all business interests to ensure continued probity while in government.

There should be a rule, precluding the subsequent employment of a member of an elected official's family to a paying position under his or her jurisdiction.

Also, all government contracts, except in specially defined situations, must be by a closed bid that is open to all members of the public meeting the industry standard or certified as such in the relevant trade or profession.

Indeed, a committee of the federal, or as the case may be, the state legislature should formulate and articulate broad and far reaching guidelines to be used by respective administrative agencies in the regulation of all government contracts and other procurement transactions.

The Domestic Revenue Collection Authority should be accorded full investigative and prosecuting powers over all persons, including elected officials, and even the estate of a decedent person, and made subject only to the general investigative powers of the federal parliament (or the state, as the case may be) .

Without a doubt, there should be some legal reform. For one thing, only persons with legal training should prosecute cases, even before Magistrate Courts. There is a clear situation of conflict when the police department that investigates crimes, and thus with a vested interest in securing convictions (being the theoretical accuser), is also permitted to prosecute those allegations of criminality.

Another matter of concern should be the recognition of those who have contributed well to general, including legal scholarship. This kind of award should not be made like a title but an annual recognition of those who have really given of themselves to others, rather than the mere fetish for tide that many aspirants to the tide of Senior Advocate of Nigeria are motivated by.

For real probity, while the president would appoint the attorney general, subject to senate approval, the attorney-general should not be a member of the President's cabinet, but made independent from it.

Indeed, as the chief law officer of the state, it might even be meet to make this an elective office on a non-party basis, with terms staggered from those of the executive so that the attorney general need not be politically affiliated, nor hostile to the executive, but mandated to protect our constitution from abuse at the risk of defeat at the polls should he not be diligent.

An arrangement like this would have avoided the appearance of impropriety that hung over the 2.8 Billion naira scandal at NNPC in the late 1970s and legions of other scandals subsequent thereto.

We certainly should improve the recording of testimony in our courts, and dispense with the sole reliance on the tired hands of some of our older judges who must write in long hands when the entire event could be tape recorded, and (or) a stenographer employed to keep a continuous record of every comment.

These are modern times. Let us upgrade our legal practice to meet the growing demands of the times. Some-one should turn on the microphones in our Courts. They are already paid for!

Additionally, like they have in some states in the United States, at least for some judicial positions, it may indeed be time to consider making some judicial positions elective.

Clearly, this has its draw backs. However, one advantage would be to free the elected judicial officer from feeling that he or she is beholden to a governor or president who appointed him or her, should there be a close case involving the interests of such executive officials (past or present). Our courts should never be allowed to settle personal vendettas. Retroactive military decrees make a mockery of the very notion of the rule of law.

Our courts must, and be seen to accord everyone with equal treatment before the law. Otherwise, the law would lose its moral force, and our justice system would become a mockery and a farce.

There should be no room in our jails for a single political prisoner of conscience that has not broken a written law. Our courts must dispense justice timely, without preference or prejudice towards any religious, political or personal views of anyone, whether for past deeds, or present misdemeanors.

Ours is not a religious, but a secular state. The state therefore has no business promoting or suppressing any religion. It should therefore permit private individuals to plan the annual pilgrimage whether to Mecca, or to Jerusalem.

What the government owes law abiding citizens who desire to make such a noble trip is not to put obstacles in their ways. In the same respect it over-reaches itself by expending scarce public resources to discount such private religious decisions when much of our social and economic infrastructures remain in dire need of repair and massive upgrading.

It is a worthy cause for a believer to prepare for the life hereafter when he or she meets the creator. However it is an equally urgent task for any elected government to ensure that while alive in this world as we know it, life is made substantially worthy of living for the tax paying, law abiding citizen. That is not asking for too much. Or is it?

One final comment on public healthcare has to be made here. It is trite to state that the good things in life are not always free. Consequently, employers that are anxious to profit from the labor of a healthy workforce must help contribute towards its wellbeing.

A nation that wants to prosper must be prepared to invest in the welfare of its youth who are the leaders of tomorrow. A society that also fails to cater for its aged can never inspire loyalty in its youths.

Another urgent issue is the unambiguous resolution of which branch of the government has the power of the purse. In civilized democracies, that power is invested in the legislature.

This is critical to inter-governmental checks and balances, and must be jealously guarded in order to stem the tide of executive abuse and administrative corruption currently evidenced by the unregulated manner in which government officials routinely dip into the national till to make arbitrary withdrawals for dubious expenses and gifts without any concern about accountability or even budgetary discipline.

To close, I disagree with the generalized contention that people just want a free ride. Most citizens are reluctant to pay taxes and other fees (i.e. new expressway toll gate fees) only when they feel the money is either being diverted to private pockets or misspent on irresponsible projects, or both.

Also, once they are given a say on whether and when to increase taxes and fees, as expressed directly by their votes, or by their elected officials whom they can vote out (in a free and fair electoral process at regulated intervals), it would be found that what people want most of all is a responsive government that delivers and levels with them.

Any aspiring leader that tells the nation that we would arrive at where we desire without overhauling our ineffectual economic system (especially the tighter regulation of our internal revenue generation and collection mechanisms) as opposed to merely waiting every month for some oil sales 'allocations' from the federal account is either ignorant untruthful, or thoroughly misinformed. If any of the above is true, then such an aspirant should either go back to the drawing board, or get a real job!

...OAU, AU, UAC, UNITED STATES OF AFRICA OR WHATEVER.... PAN AFRICANISM MUST BE REVISITED

It continues to be a source of shame that most of the countries in Africa are in worse shape than they were pre-colonial independence. There is no legitimate reason why Africans (of all races, religion and creed) should not be able to prosper on the most amazingly beautiful and rich continent under the sun.

Given the current state of affairs, including the national and multi-national (business) forces arrayed against this salutary quest, getting the continent back on track would require imaginative new leadership and a collective fastidiousness for the good life.

We should unequivocally reject being patronized and demand that we be treated with respect. History would attest to the fact that no real quarter will ever be offered to us.

None should be expected again by or from us. The rules of the game were changed in mid—course. Such is the immorality that has been accorded world-wide legitimacy as "informed self interest."

It is legitimate for other countries or people to set self-serving goals and to attain those goals. African countries should set goals larger than the egos of some of its erstwhile "life presidents" who's terms were recently hastened to reach the logically inglorious end.

I am reminded of a Yoruba proverb which goes as follows: AGBA JO OWO LA FI NSO YA. The essence of this is that when we are united, we are able to speak and act with more assurance. That some leaders in the early days of the continent were not able to reason with Nkrumah is at best mystifying.

Since the majority of the diffident heads of states on the continent is now adept at the political game of "follow the leader", one would hope that considering that the trend now in Europe is towards a united political and economic bloc (CALLED THE 'EU'), hopefully, our accidental leaders will emulate something imaginative and positive for a change; even though it is about forty years overdue.

More so, it was an indigenous idea that was previously pooh-poohed by the west who didn't want us to truly come away from under the bondage of our sad heritage.

For too long, many African Countries were no more than dispensable client-states to other outside powers.

It is a matter of common knowledge that much of the self-imposed and foreign engineered economic and political malaise afflicting the continent only serve to make Africa more vulnerable to indirect foreign domination. **The decision to permanently subjugate the continent recently reached new heights.**

African leadership only needs to open its eyes to discern that the continent is being re-colonized all over again through debt entrapment. The irony of it is that the bulk of the borrowed money was handed over to those who were hell-bent on robbing the continent blind, only to reinvest it in the economies of the lending nations.

Now they have us where they really want us. **As one of my favorite comedians aptly put it, it is a dog eat dog world, and we are stuck in milk bone underwear. We are getting screwed!**

Consequently, in a futile endeavor to honor our debts, foreign creditors who in fact are mere agents of outside political powers dictate both the economic and social policies of most African countries under the guise of "debt restructuring". Our mind-set and collective psyche have been restructured all right. We've been had! The continent is therefore caught in a vicious circle.

The various economies have been bashed from within, and sabotaged from without. Many countries on the continent are desperate for capital. Foreign institutions and governments are thought to be the only game in town.

The thing we hate most, it turns out, are often the things necessary for survival. Someone should remind these leaders that there is something called internal borrowing by selling government Notes or Bonds to individuals or companies at reasonable interest rates.

Ultimately, you get much of the same resources without mortgaging national sovereignty in the process. They call us third world countries with barely understated condescension.

We should not glorify this by clinging to the alibi of an arrested intellectual development. Africa is now hostage to the defeatist sensibilities of its leaders that are now burdened by their armor of inferiority complex which some of them wear with eminent ignorance.

There is now a near cynical admonishment by these same leaders who would be mercilessly vicious when it suits their purpose.

They are suing for peace and stability in the face of imminent defeat. However, what is nominal peace, when the definition of their peace is Africa's collective subjugation and truncated growth. Indeed, what is peace without human dignity?

What is peace without honor? Whose peace do they seek to preserve when your sensibilities have been ravaged, and they have mocked and destroyed the very things you value most.

They forgot the biblical admonishment that those who ravage their own homes will surely inherit the wind. Presently, the wind begins to blow. Blow, baby blow!

In the interim, the continent is getting suffocated by fawning clowns that cloak themselves in tattered and tarnished national flags, and issuing empty nationalistic rhetoric that neither feed our young ones, nor stem the tide of monumental corruption that begins to stink to high heavens.

We must wake up to the realities of the times. We must aim to deter further economic and political aggressions and manipulations both from within and from without. We must not aim to provoke a fight for the sheer joy of it. Lord knows we are probably primed for one.

Blind anger does not work. We must thus channel our energies constructively. We must be rid of the dead woods that currently hold sway in many parts of Africa.

For too long, we have been cursed with a redundant army of self-serving leaders who need our continued goodwill and accommodation more than we need theirs. They cling desperately to power and hold on to our receding patience like a deadening fatigue one carries around like a cloak.

Like their erstwhile colonial instructors, they recognize that a better informed population will prove more unmanageable with time.

Consequently, they have therefore cast the bulk of an entire generation into perpetual intellectual darkness and enduring servitude. However, if they think they can pull this off much longer, then they should think again. Naturally, they would dream up schemes.

Any notion that this nonsense will linger longer is only an indication that, in their desperation, they are not only dreaming the impossible dreams, they are dreaming it in Technicolor.

The time is long overdue for efficacious restoratives. We must apply them ourselves. We must be prepared to abide some pain.
We must be willing to hurt, if it will stop a greater pain. We welcome sincere support from all quarters, even our tormentors of the very recent past.

However, we would determine and channel our own course the way we see it. Liberal altruism is one thing, patronizing and paternalistic conceit is quite another.

Those who have ears should listen and listen well. We mean no race, religion or nation any ill. We would however respond in kind to any untoward gesture from any quarter. Unlike the staid leadership whose time has passed, we will vigorously pursue the African destiny with pride and focus. We would demand of our new leaders the courage to make tough choices.

Life, after all is itself a daring adventure, or it is nothing at all. It is going to be a painful transition. The disease hurts, but so does the surgeon's knife. For our future socio-political health, it is obvious which choice we would make.

We have been failed by the previous generation of leaders. We must not end up being impari-delicto (equally guilty!). Having recognized their failings and the reasons explaining them, we have exhausted our alibi for failure. We are not limited by the myopic horizon of youth. We are getting up in years. And time continues to pass.

We have a responsibility to the coming generations. We have a duty to brush off at least some of the dirt, so that there is less to offend when their time comes. This goal requires both vision and courage. But there is no vision without faith. And even real courage translates into a determination to go on and to do what needs to be done in spite of one's fears.

Indeed, it becomes clear that we are liable to feel the pain before we eventually feel the healing.

It is a disgrace to an entire continent (and race) when it cannot do anything it feels is in its interest without seeking a tacit approval from some outside institution or government

Having the Organization of African Unity is certainly better than nothing. However, it is an open secret that even the organization is at best a toothless bulldog! Even its occasional barks are sporadic, selective and rather ephemeral.

Let me therefore reiterate this proposal again. We must creatively explore the gradual reconstitution of the various countries in Africa, first into a confederation of states, with the hope of a potential future merger of sorts. Exploration of this idea should begin in earnest.

If the matter is sincerely pursued by the more affluent countries in the continent with a clear arrangement which ensures a substantially equal partnership with even the smallest of the merging countries (i.e. the use of electoral college and having each current entity have the same number of senators or governor-generals in addition to a separate body that accurately reflects representation based on shifting population patters like you have with all the uniting colonies that formed the current United States), it will eliminate the artificial concerns of possible domination, yet having a compelling economic and political appeal to all concerned.

Those who are likely to stand in the way of this progressive move would be the cadre of the current leadership and their army of apologists who are liable to construe this development in its narrow context of foreshadowing their loss of political hegemony and the perquisites that go with it.

A continent wide campaign should therefore be waged to ensure that, unlike other efforts at racial awakening, the real people are allowed a say on what shape their future destinies should take. It would be legitimate therefore to hold referendums after the people are better informed of what is at stake, and what the choices are, including the risks and rewards.

Nay-Sayers, no doubt, will abound. They too are entitled to be heard. However, as Henry Ford, the late automobile pioneer was quoted as saying, "say you can, say you can't, either way you'd be right".

Consequently, I feel comfortable in saying that we as a people would be limited only by the degree of our daring, and the magnitude of our collective imaginative fancy. So, the inevitable success that awaits such a daring would be made even sweeter where, (as we are now) burdened by formidable adversity.

Actually, no force on earth that I recognize is able to deter and permanently deny the very yearnings of a people who, collectively, have resolved themselves to fulfilling those aspirations.

This call to unity is not only germane for the economic emancipation of Africa, it is critical to its political stability. This resolve would magnify the uniqueness and pride of the African, yet dissolving the walls of artificial differences erected to destroy the unity and similarities in humankind.

The demand to loudly reaffirm our humanity is not designed to diminish the humanity of others. However, such affirmations would, at the very least, remove and elevate us from the back stage seat of world cut-throat competition where we've been consigned for centuries now, to the very beginnings of real racial equality and respect, no questions asked.

As unjust as it may sound, this demanded respect must, in the final analysis, be earned.

When you consider now that there are hundreds, nay thousands of Americans striving to learn Japanese (and more recently, Chinese) on account of the seemingly meteoric rise of Japan and China and that China is now the chief creditor nation to the otherwise invincible U.S of A, you cannot but recall that it was just a few years ago that children were still being weaned on the marvel of the implied superiority of the Anglo-Saxon in every aspect of human endeavor, and people of Oriental descent were pooh-poohed and summarily dismissed with flourish.

If we demand and work for true change, we would encourage people of sterling qualities to come forward to lead us to the symbolic Promised Land. The continent desperately needs leaders who would put the interests of the young and the coming generations above ephemeral and self-serving schemes.

Let us encourage those who are still ambivalent that there is a better appeal in being participants of a bigger and stronger Africa than the uncertainties that has and probably will continue to beset the current small, disparate, indiscriminately put together volatile and angry warring communities being egged on to the very edge of self immolation by the idiocy of leaders who divide rather than unite and heal.

It is better for our people to live for a better Africa, than to die on behalf (or in the hands) of a despotic madman clinging desperately to a marginal hegemony.

It is significant that the **CEO OF GOOGLE in the United States**, for example, controls a budget (and international communication mechanism) that impacts the lives and economic wellbeing of more people than does many so called life Presidents of several African countries put together.

What our leaders should do is politely sever the demeaning umbilical cord of neo-colonial paternalism and grow up.

They should realize that they certainly have more in common with fellow African Countries than their unequal fawning relationship with prior colonial exploiters.

Those with vision and purpose are countries who took advantage of their Islamic heritage by joining the Arab League, especially on account of the lack of focus and direction exhibited by the O.A.U. This is no time to subscribe to the continued mentorship by defunct colonial Overlords.

Consequently, I consider the so called British Commonwealth of Nations (a conglomeration of countries that have been previously ravished by imperialist Britain) a cynical British ploy to permanently make their past domination over these countries a subliminally enduring thing.

They are rubbing it in! I am aghast and find myself unable to fathom how a leader with any imagination could justify why membership in such a sorry group of peons that exists only to massage the massive British ego is more critical to national growth than working to foster a United States of Africa or an African League with some real backbone!

Again, we must never forget that Yoruba adage—"AGBA JO OWO LA FI NSOYA"—meaning, united we stand and implying that divided, we probably stand little chance. And indeed we must so stand to protect our heritage and allow our tremendous strengths to flourish.

The goal is now set. The strategies may differ. As long as we get there, what does it matter? Some now propose as a viable strategy that we should appeal to the innate morality of those who led us astray, or wickedly blocked our paths to salvation. The goal is to make them remorseful with guilt, hoping that the guilt might wear them down and deter them from their wicked ways. Balderdash!

We must hasten and strike while the iron is hot. Like the Japanese and the Chinese, we should shamelessly emulate any positive or valuable knowledge we need to make our societies function more efficiently while prudently learning from the mistakes of those that have gone before us by wisely pruning the fat from the real meat.

We must learn the rudiments and supplement same with our own unique learning in a bid to re-master a workable imperfection.

In closing, I should invite you to consider the words of **Awolowo who wrote in his book, The Problems of Africa, that much of the problems afflicting Africa, (and indeed the world) are ones in which human beings themselves can address by properly channeling their faculties and not ones in which solutions are wrought by appealing to some mystical being in the skies.**

To be sure, if religion is considered the opium of the people, then it is equally meet that they religiously demand of their leaders, those things they crave, which are at least attainable, because it has pleased God (whatever gods they believe in) to make such attainments within the immediate reach of human exertions.

We are destined to fall into forgettable ignominy and become extinct like the dinosaurs that once bestrode this earth, or unite and rise above artificial obstacles and puerile distractions to be accorded recognition duly deserved.

Consider that with the continent's tremendous human and natural resources, and imbued with the bitter knowledge of the failures of the past there really is only one way to go: first class all the way to the top, even from the depths of poverty; and forward from the backwaters of ineptitude and mediocrity.

Stay with me awhile longer. The climb ahead may be tedious, but delightful and heady, as things have gotten so bad, they can only get better.

I say to you that those who came before us probably may have viewed the rainbow as an optical illusion, and a quest to discover the beginnings of its majesty an unwholesome form of idiocy. I shamelessly confess to such idiocy. But consider for a moment that the thunderous rain is now spent, having exhausted its might in lashing and lavishing its showers on us.

Now, at the horizon, the sun begins to shine. I assure you that the brightness that illuminates as you behold the horizon is the rainbow in its full glory. Yes, we are Africans, in full colors and ready to bloom, and we are poised to reclaim our noble destiny.

—∿∿∘๑ᒒᴎᴑᴆᴎᴑᴑ∘∿∿—

Concluding Remarks

—∿∿∘๑ᒒᴎᴑᴆᴎᴑᴑ∘∿∿—

We must collectively insist on a truly representative democracy for selecting our leaders. We must never tire of making them accountable to our needs. Our people should no longer thirst while atop an oasis. Our people should no longer beg for crumbs when their place is right at the Masters' table.

WE MUST PASSIONATELY REAFFIRM OUR COMMON HUMANITY AND COLLECTIVE DESTINY. WE MUST REACH OUT TO OTHERS LESS FORTUNATE WITH EMPATHY AND PURPOSE. WE MUST, WITH HUMILITY STRIVE TO ELEVATE THE BETTER ANGELS OF OUR NATURE.

The Chinese language identifies what we call 'CRISIS' as "AN OPPORTUNITY RIDING ON A DANGEROUS WIND."

Essentially, the Chinese MENTALITY AND CULTURAL PRE-DISPOSITION is to properly focus more on the potential of making something worthwhile out of an otherwise challenging development.

We would do well to imbibe this psychological posture.

Indeed the genius and human utility exemplified with the creation of the Hoover Dam, Lake Mead and the electricity generation plant from what for decades was the destructive force of the Colorado river as it barrels through America's western desert states is a credit to visionary leadership and the dynamic human spirit of the American people.

This is a great metaphor for how those of us in Africa could own and dominate our environment and our circumstances by creating awe inspiring opportunities from natural or other human engineered challenges.

It becomes that much easier when you recognize that Nigeria for example does not have to contend with earthquakes, hurricanes, snow storms,

ice storms, or any significant inclement force of nature that would have inhibited, slowed or prevented social growth and technological advancements.

We must demand that elected leaders rediscover their collective backbone, by cultivating constructive and mutually beneficial international alliances (NOT DIFFIDENTLY WITH CAP IN HAND AS EXTRAS AT THE OCASSIONAL G-8 SUMMIT, OR BEGGING TO BE LET OFF THE HOOK FOR LOANS THEY SHOULD NEITHER HAVE TAKEN, NOR STOLEN IN THE FIRST PLACE). Rather, they should forge constructive international alliances with a measure of dignity and sensitivity to the interests of their real constituents.

Placing the nation in a position where some World Bank bureaucrats dictate national policies for an ostensibly "independent" Nation is most troubling and totally intolerable.

Monies collected as national loans by African leaders are typically misappropriated or secreted ABROAD IN PRIVATE ACCOUNTS for personal use. Sometimes the monies are held for a while to quickly generate substantial interests for their own use before the principal amount is released for its intended use. In the meantime, they consciously mortgage the future of a state or an entire nation, merely to satisfy a personal greed. This is clearly as heinous as any crime against humanity. Think about it!

With diminished resources, the country is thus deprived of the ability, for example, to buy hospital equipments, ambulances and firefighting vehicles that could save lives.

JUST THINK ABOUT THE DOMINO EFFECT OF EVERY FRAUDULENT OR UNCOMPLETED CONTRACT. PLEASE TAKE A MOMENT TO DO THIS. NOW IMAGINE HOW THOROUGHLY MODERNIZED AND PLEASANT NIGERIA WOULD BE TODAY HAD LEADERS INVESTED WITH THE NATIONAL TRUST ACTED WITH HONOR AND A SENSE OF PATRIOTISM.

I ASSURE YOU, THINGS CAN EVEN GET WORSE IF WE DON'T ACT NOW. REMEMBER, DURING BABANGIDA'S TIME, PEOPLE

FELT THINGS COULD NOT GET WORSE. WELL, THEN CAME ABACHA. GET THE PICTURE? THESE THIEVES IN HIGH PLACES HAVE "TASTED BLOOD" MANY OF THEM GENUINELY FEEL THAT NOTHING WILL EVER INHIBIT OR SANCTION THEM FOR THEIR STEALING PUBLIC FUNDS. SO THEY DO IT WITH IMPUNITY. UNLESS THIS TREND IS EFFECTIVELY CHALLENGED AND STOPPED, THE FUTURE OF THIS COUNTRY MAY BE MORE NIGHMARISH THAN ANY OF US MAY BE WILLING TO IMAGINE NOW, EVEN IN OUR WILDEST MOMENTS OF TERROR.

NO FOREIGN NATION WILL COME TO OUR AID, SOLELY OUT OF THE GOODNESS OF ITS HEART UNLESS ITS INTERESTS HAPPEN TO COINCIDE WITH OURS. SO, FOLKS SHOULD SNAP OUT OF THE PREVAILING DELUSION THAT, AT THE BASEST LEVEL, FOLKS IN THE OTHER CAPITALS OF THE WORLD ARE PRE-OCCUPIED WITH WORRYING ABOUT OUR BEST INTERESTS. ALL WE HAVE IS US AND OUR DETERMINATION NOT TO SETTLE FOR A WRETCHED LIFE OF MEDIOCRITY AND MISSED OPPORTUNITIES.

I MEAN, DO WE NOT DESERVE THE SAME QUALITY OF LIFE THAT IS ENJOYED BY THE AVERAGE AMERICAN, OR THE AVERAGE FRENCH OR ENGLISH MAN?

SHOULD IT MATTER THAT WE ARE OF A DIFFERENT SKIN COLOR? IF NOT, THEN WHY ARE WE NOT ACTING AS IF WE DESERVE THOSE THINGS? IS IT FEAR? IF SO, WE SHOULD INQUIRE, FEAR OF WHAT?

WE ARE ALL GOING TO DIE. EVEN THE FEARSOME ABACHA EVENTUALLY MET HIS PHYSICAL DEMISE.

ARE WE CONCEDING THAT THESE NATIONAL CROOKS ARE SMARTER OR MORE RESOURCEFUL THAN WE ARE? I RATHER DOUBT IT VERY MUCH. WE JUST NEED TO ACT WITH A COLLECTIVE RESOLVE THAT ENOUGH IS ENOUGH!

IF WE THROW A FEW OF THEM IN JAIL FOR STEALING PUBLIC FUNDS, BELIEVE ME IT WILL SEND THE RIGHT MESSAGE

THAT THIS TYPE OF NONESENSE WILL NO LONGER BE TOLERATED.

THAT IS HOW THINGS WORK IN THE BETTER ORGANIZED SOCIETIES WE HAVE SOMETIMES TRIED TO SELECTIVELY EMULATE IN THE PAST.

Further, by way of convenient example, the United States which is the most dominant economy in the world is a key nation with which a leader would need to cultivate, or expand upon an existing positive relationship, because it is potentially beneficial to both.

To that end, for example, in this new vision of a dynamic nation that looks out for the best interest of its people, the new generation of leaders should readily be a friend of **Bill Clinton's America that is strong, yet humble enough to apologize for the devastating effects of slavery** while being genuinely inclusive.

The next generation of leaders should be a friend to **George Herbert Walker Bush's stated vision of America that is great, yet kinder and gentler.**

They should be a friend of **Ronald Reagan's America** that is unpretentious about projecting a moral certitude about Man's right to freedom from oppression.

Our new leaders should most certainly be **a friend of Jimmy Carter's (and Barack Obama's) America that recognizes that the world shares a collective destiny and seeks to promote the very best virtues that unite us towards that common end.**

The next generation of leaders should be a friend of **Reverend Martin Luther King Junior's** dream of America that continues to strive to live up to the true meaning of its creed that all Men are created equal (and therefore should be treated as equals).

They should of course be a friend **of Malcolm X's America** that concedes the imperfections in all of us, yet defiantly and with a valiant spirit, rises above human imperfections to inspire others to great heights.

Ultimately, my fervent dream is that future African leaders would be a friend of Akinwale, Temitayo and Akintoye's America because as the dominant empire of this unique age of "democracy" and "freedom," there is still a measure of true idealistic innocence to it that it might yet do more good during its time, than all the other great empires that once bestrode the earth.

And the world should hopefully continue to insist that all great Nations give equal respect to other people's right to advance legitimate goals that are beneficial to them as sovereign entities.

To that end, folks who currently represent the international interests of a country like Nigeria should take note. We have been watching their performance over the years, and we have not been overly impressed.

Most citizens living abroad would happily return home but for the cynical refusal of the current cadre of corrupt officials to allow the emergence of a society that is truly under the rule of law and representative democracy, not the dangerously unpredictable whims of a few ruling clique.

It is that kind of environment that will ensure that reasonable business risks can be taken based on predictable and established rules of general application. NOT THE PREVAILING "man-know-man" CULTURE THAT HAS, OVER THE YEARS, MOVED NIGERIA UP THE LIST AS ONE OF THE TOP THREE MOST CORRUPT COUNTRIES IN THE WHOLE WORLD!

So much for the anti-corruption crusade! Indeed, it has been said that, thanks to the moral and financial support of many who were based abroad, the Nigerian economy and the very welfare of millions might have been in greater peril over the last decade or so.

However, Nigeria cannot attain its true potential when many who are clearly its best educated, and resourceful are compelled by circumstances to stay away from the political madness and orchestrated social chaos and near anarchy.

Those who love this country must work in a coordinated fashion to ensure that the enabling environment promptly develops to encourage even more of our able citizens to begin to repatriate some of their financial and intellectual wealth back to the country.

MAKE NO MISTAKE. THEIR EXPECTED CONTRIBUTIONS ARE URGENTLY NEEDED. AND IF DEPLOYED IN A WELL ORCHESTRATED MANNER, IT COULD MARKEDLY HELP TO TURN AROUND THE ECONOMIC FORTUNES OF THE ENTIRE NATION RATHER EXPEDITIOUSLY.

AFTER ALL, THE STOLEN MONIES SPIRITED AWAY BY OUR THIEVING LEADERS AND KEPT IN FOREIGN ACCOUNTS ARE NOT DOING ANYTHING TO ADVANCE OUR ECONOMY.

In the meantime, many Nigerians abroad (as some of the information referenced in this Book reveal) are actually doing great things. And some are forming valuable alliances that will benefit Nigeria, indeed Africa for generations yet to come.

A few examples of those have been briefly touched upon, to hopefully inspire others, and imbue the rest of us with a sense of hope and pride.

YES, WE ARE SOMEBODY. THE ACCOMPLISHMENTS BY MANY AFRICANS ABROAD GIVE ME THE CONFIDENCE THAT IF GIVEN THE OPPORTUNITY, AND THE CONDUCIVE ENVIRONMENT, MANY OF THOSE CURRENTLY LIVING ABROAD CAN RADICALLY HELP IN THE QUEST TO IMPROVE THE LIVES OF THE CITIZENS OF OUR POTENTIALLY GREAT NATION (EITHER IN THE AREA OF EFFECTIVE NATIONAL PLANNING, COMMERCE, EDUCATION, AGRICULTURE, RESOURCE MANAGEMENT, NATIONAL SECURITY AND JUSTICE)

Of course, all that glitters is not gold. It is of course sometimes painful to see how many of our citizens employ their talent to benefit their current overseas 'HOSTS', while the nation hungers for their talents. It is even sadder to see very qualified people deprived of opportunities to significantly contribute, both back home and abroad, thereby depriving millions of their talents, either as Scientists, Educators, Engineers, Doctors, Lawyers, Nation Builders, Artists, Inspirational thinkers, Nurses, Entertainers and the like.

The likes of Abacha and Babangida were certainly happy to see many leave. It somewhat reduced the stridency of the opposition to their misrule. Fortunately for the country, many of those who traveled abroad used the opportunity to improve themselves and to reflect on how things could work better for Nigeria.

It will truly be a great day when all that learning and all that valuable perspective is returned home and brought to bear on the various challenges that currently confront the nation.

Hopefully, that new age of fresh ideas, dynamism and selfless leadership is almost upon us. WE SHOULD BEGIN TO READJUST OUR THINKING AND OUR RESPECTIVE TIME TABLES ABOUT SLOWLY RETURNING HOME TO CONTRIBUTE OUR MODEST QUOTA. WE OWE IT TO OUR CHILDREN AND THEIR CHILDREN'S CHILDREN AS A MATTER OF RACIAL PRIDE.

There is no great meaning in the routine and the tedium of our toil except for the impact they may have on others

CLOSING WITH THE 'ZEN MASTER'S' PERSPECTIVE

The following represents my spin on this cautionary tale. A young man captured a wild horse and rode it triumphantly into the village to general applause.

When the village Zen master was told about this development, his only response was, "WE'LL SEE"

Not too long after this, the young man fell and broke both of his legs while riding his new horse. Being so popular and celebrated, the whole village commiserated with him.

When the villagers suggested to the Zen Master that perhaps the horse was more of a curse given the young man's severe injuries, his only response was, "WE'LL SEE"

Before the young man sufficiently recovered from his severe injuries war broke out with the neighboring village. The war went so badly that they conscripted all the young men in the village to fight.

Because of his injuries, the young man was exempted from the conscription into the army. When a number of the villagers were commenting to the Zen Master how lucky the young man was for avoiding military conscription because of his broken legs, again, the Zen Master's only comment was "WE'LL SEE"

A LOT HAS BEEN WRITTEN, SAID AND DONE BY SO MANY TO POSITIVELY TURN AFRICA'S (AND NIGERIA'S) FORTUNE AROUND.

SO, WITH RESPECT TO HOW THINGS WILL EVENTUALLY SHAPE OUT IN THE COMING YEARS FOR NIGERIA AND AFRICA, ALL ANYONE CAN PRUDENTLY SAY IS,
"WE'LL SEE"

SOME IMPORTANT INSPIRATIONAL REFERENCES

WISDOM OF THE TAO—when you change the way you look at things, the things you look at change!

THE TAO TE CHING is a collection of 81 verses authored by LAO-TZU a Chinese Prophet some 25 centuries ago and translated into English by a number of distinguished writers.

THE TAO TE CHING ESSENTIALLY MEANS LIVING WISELY AND APPLYING THE GREAT WISDOM OF NATURE.